COLLEEN SWINDOLL THOMPSON

Reframing Life

Focusing on God
When Life Gets Sideways

REVISED &
EXPANDED

From the Bible-Teaching Ministry of
CHARLES R. SWINDOLL

REFRAMING LIFE
Focusing on God When Life Gets Sideways
From the Bible-Teaching Ministry of Charles R. Swindoll

Charles R. Swindoll has devoted his life to the accurate, practical teaching and application of God's Word and His grace. A pastor at heart, Chuck has served as senior pastor to congregations in Massachusetts, California, and Texas. Since 1998, he has served as the founder and senior pastor-teacher of Stonebriar Community Church in Frisco, Texas, but Chuck's listening audience extends far beyond a local church body. As a leading program in Christian broadcasting since 1979, *Insight for Living* airs in major Christian radio markets around the world, reaching people groups in languages they can understand. Chuck's extensive writing ministry has also served the body of Christ worldwide, and his leadership as president and now chancellor of Dallas Theological Seminary has helped prepare and equip a new generation of men and women for ministry. Chuck and Cynthia, his partner in life and ministry, have four grown children, ten grandchildren, and seven great-grandchildren.

Copyright © 2016 by Insight for Living Ministries
Revised and Expanded Edition, Copyright © 2018 by Insight for Living Ministries

All rights are reserved worldwide under international copyright conventions. No portion of *Reframing Life: Focusing on God When Life Gets Sideways* may be reproduced, stored in a retrieval system, or transmitted in any form or by any means—electronic, mechanical, photocopy, recording, or any other system now known or yet to be invented—except for brief quotations in printed reviews, without the prior written permission of the copyright holders. **Please purchase only authorized electronic editions and do not participate in or encourage electronic piracy of copyrightable materials.** Inquiries should be addressed to Insight for Living Ministries, Rights and Permissions, Post Office Box 1050, Frisco, Texas, 75034-1050 or sent by e-mail to rights@insight.org or made online at www.insight.org/permissions.

Published By: IFL Publishing House, A Division of Insight for Living Ministries,
Post Office Box 5000, Frisco, Texas 75034-0055

Editor in Chief: Cynthia Swindoll, President and Chief Executive Officer, Insight for Living Ministries
Executive Vice President: Bryce Klabunde, Th.M., Dallas Theological Seminary; D. Min., Western Seminary
Writer: Colleen Swindoll Thompson, B.A., Communication, Trinity International University
Communications Specialist: Kathryn Robertson, M.A., English, Hardin-Simmons University
Copy Editors: Alicia Brumley, B.S., Interdisciplinary Studies, Texas A&M University
Jim Craft, M.A., English, Mississippi College; M.A., Christian Studies, Dallas Theological Seminary
Project Manager, Publishing: StacieNicole Simmons, B.A., Literature, State University of New York at Purchase; M.A., History, American University
Proofreader: Alicia Brumley, B.S., Interdisciplinary Studies, Texas A&M University
Designer: Dameon Runnels, B.A., Art—Mass Media; B.A., Mass Communications, Grambling State University
Design adapted from Laura Dubroc, B.F.A., Advertising Design, University of Louisiana at Lafayette
Production Artist: Nancy Gustine, B.F.A., Advertising Art, University of North Texas

Unless otherwise identified, Scripture quotations are taken from the Holy Bible, New Living Translation, copyright © 1996, 2004, 2015 by Tyndale House Foundation. Used by permission of Tyndale House Publishers, Inc., Carol Stream, Illinois 60188. All rights reserved.

Scripture quotations marked (NASB) are taken from the New American Standard Bible® (NASB). Copyright © 1960, 1962, 1963, 1968, 1971, 1972, 1973, 1975, 1977, 1995 by The Lockman Foundation. Used by permission. www.Lockman.org

An effort has been made to locate sources and obtain permission where necessary for the quotations used in this book. In the event of any unintentional omission, a modification will gladly be incorporated in future printings.

ISBN: 978-1-62655-019-3
Printed in the United States of America

Table of Contents

A Letter from Chuck and Cynthia

Cynthia and I have never been prouder of our daughter Colleen than we are today.

Though Colleen might tell you differently, she is stronger and faster than ever before. The Lord has been molding her character through her circumstances—including a surgery that welded her spine together with titanium rods, several surgical screws, and excruciating physical therapy—so that she would be tougher and more resilient spiritually.

Colleen has been and continues to be a tireless, attentive caretaker for our grandson with many special needs as he transitions into adulthood. She has supported our granddaughter as she married her sweetheart . . . and helped pack our other grandson's suitcases as he ventured off to college, which included a trip to China! Her life story includes pages on abuse, divorce, chronic pain, and the devastating heartbreak of a failed justice system . . . as well as chapters dedicated to the joys and struggles of remarriage and parenting in a blended family. With each hurdle life has placed before her, Colleen has found the strength, responsiveness, and agility to leap forward, pressing onward.

I don't mention these events to evoke pity or impress you. Rather, I mention them to give testimony to two truths:

- God is faithful in the best of times, the worst of times, and through all of life's transitions.

- The book you hold in your hand is written by someone who gets it; she's been where you are.

Colleen reminds us of the words written by the Old Testament prophet Habakkuk:

> *The Sovereign* LORD *is my strength!*
> *He makes me as surefooted as a deer,*
> *able to tread upon the heights.*
> (Habakkuk 3:19)

After describing withering fig trees and fruitless grapevines, Habakkuk expressed his confidence in the Lord as his strength. The prophet's lips trembled and his legs shook as he envisioned God's righteous judgment upon the nations.

But after seeing what he saw, Habakkuk's trembling legs didn't buckle. Instead, they became strong and sure. Though his circumstances had not changed, his focus had. If you will, Habakkuk *reframed* his perspective.

The chapters of *Reframing Life* were forged in 5 a.m. wake-up calls and midnight-hour emergency room visits—in moments of gut-level wrestling and weariness and wondering. This book is filled with lessons on how to run strong-legged in spite of knee-weakening hurdles like loneliness, disappointment, fear, and exhaustion. Colleen's a good coach, guiding you without an ounce of pretension but with plenty of energy, humility, wisdom, empathy, and humor.

We promise Colleen's book won't leave you in the doldrums. Our daughter's joy is infectious, and her sense of humor is laugh-out-loud funny. (Don't read this book in the library or you'll get hushed!)

As Colleen will explain much better than we can, to run well is to focus not on the hurdles but on the Author and Finisher of our faith, Jesus. Colleen's sure-footed faith and relentless compassion, especially in times of struggle, serve as a reflection of Christlikeness that continues to inspire us. I'm confident it will do the same for you.

Chuck and Cynthia Swindoll

Chuck and Cynthia Swindoll

About Me

Once upon a time, I strived for perfection. I read every how-to book, wishing a little fairy dust could sprinkle away problems I couldn't control. Everything changed the day I found my daughter's suicide note scratched on a piece of wrinkled paper. Not long after, my first marriage ended in a messy divorce. I became a single parent with three children, each facing serious challenges. My youngest was diagnosed with more disabilities than there are letters in the alphabet, my middle son had learning challenges and struggled in school, and my daughter was self-harming and severely depressed. The picture-perfect family I envisioned had fallen apart.

Years have passed. My kids have healed and grown. My youngest will live with disabilities for the rest of his life unless the Lord chooses otherwise. I continue to devour books on everything from spiritual development to neurobiological advancements, but my motivation for reading has shifted. Instead of trying to fix and control everything, I've learned to embrace that life is broken, and people are hurting. BUT in the midst of it all, God is always good and faithfully working—even though it often feels otherwise.

I'm honored to serve as the director of Reframing Ministries at Insight for Living Ministries. *Reframing* means choosing to look at life through a different lens, one that is accurate, honest, and aligned with God's Word. When we change our perspectives, we see life in new ways. It's all about coming to the end of ourselves and embracing God's plan. Remembering His good plan requires we release ours to Him.

My desire is that you will find help, hope, healing, and a lot of humor in the pages of this book and the other resources I helped put together. Reframing Ministries is specifically designed with you in mind—not the "almost perfect," "put together" you, but the you that is human and shows up just as you are. More than anything, I pray our time together will remind you how valuable you are and that God isn't done writing your story.

In 1993, Colleen graduated with a degree in communications and a double-minor in education and psychology. Colleen's passion is to connect and encourage caregivers, domestic-abuse survivors, the disabled, and all those struggling with challenges of faith and life. She also loves to read and apply God's Word through writing, speaking at events and conferences, and teaching Bible studies. Colleen's favorite time is spent with her husband, Toban, whom she married in 2009. Together, they share five grown children, two of whom are married. Calling themselves the "Blended Bunch," they love playing games, making music, and filling their home with a lot of laughter. When time permits, she enjoys working in her yard, exercising, and reading. Colleen and Toban reside in Frisco, Texas.

How to Get the Most from This Book

Sirens wailed as the ambulance sped through the newly developed, swanky suburban neighborhood.

It was the first weekend of summer. In typical southern fashion, smoke curled from barbeque grills loaded with layers of sizzling hamburger patties and hot dogs; homemade ice cream churned close by. Young couples chatted about vacation plans, their kids fully occupied with water games and splashing contests in the pool. Between the giggles and squeals, cicadas hummed.

Then a mother's scream consumed all other sounds. Her terror was suffocating. Her 4-year-old daughter lay lifeless at the bottom of the pool. Panic coursed through the backyard. The mother dove in, pulling the girl up to the surface. One man called 9 1 1. Another performed CPR. All prayed with the girl's parents, pleading for God to save her life.

The parents' trembling fear turned into elated relief as their daughter coughed and sputtered back to life. She had been rescued! Praise the Lord! He had heard their cries!

But this God-fearing, loving couple couldn't have imagined how their lives had instantly changed. Their daughter had been saved at a cost: the accident had permanently and severely disabled her. The damage was irreversible.

In the days since time stood still around that pool, she has not improved. Unless God heals her, this will be the family's "new normal" until Jesus returns or calls them home.

When crises, unexpected events, changes, and loss hit us, most Christians pray. We pray for healing, hope, strength, and relief. We mean our prayers; our hearts are earnest. But rarely do we realize that our prayers carry expectations that God will answer in certain ways. All we know is He is good, and we are faithful. How could we expect less than to pull through with healing, relief, and a wonderful testimony? When the Lord doesn't provide what we expected, we begin to ask questions:

- *Did we pray hard enough?*

- *Did God hear our prayers?*

- *Should we have prayed differently?*

- *How could a good God allow _____ to happen?*

- *What could I have done differently?*

- *Who caused this to happen?*

- *Is there really a God after all?*

Unfortunately, there's no map or formula for finding a "new normal." Circumstances we couldn't have planned and changes we never expected (and even some that we did) affect us in every way—physically, mentally, emotionally, relationally, and spiritually. My guess is, you know what I'm talking about. Perhaps you've been on the other side too—wanting to help but not knowing how. Tragically, most Christians *want* to help but aren't equipped to do so. We try but ultimately end up saying or doing things that make matters worse.

If you're hurting, grappling with the unexpected, grieving a loss, or learning a new normal . . . if you're struggling to find your way, teetering on the edge, fighting to catch your breath, or simply tired of feeling unfulfilled, exhausted, disappointed, and conflicted . . . this book is for you. If you're wanting to offer support to others, this book is also for you.

This volume represents what I wish I had long ago. It's a book born from *years* of searching for a healing process—one created and organized for those trying to move forward. Think of it as your survival guide back to sanity. The chapters are short, thought-provoking, and soul-searching. Best of all, they give you permission to examine your faith as you may never have before.

What you won't find in these pages are shame and guilt. This book will be an affirming voice, cheering you on in your journey and being a shoulder to cry on when you're not up to running. This book, like the healing process, isn't a sprint. It's not meant to be read from cover to cover. It's designed for you to work through at your own pace. No one can hurry through healing, because healing takes time.

I've named the process described in this book "reframing." The word *reframing* originated with cognitive behavioral specialists working in the field of psychology. It means choosing to look at life through a different lens, to alter our perspectives, to find opportunity and purpose as we learn new ways of living. For believers, reframing means choosing to see our lives through the lens of God's Word. It requires engaging our heads, our hearts, and our habits. To facilitate healing, we must learn to think differently, address our emotions honestly, and cultivate new daily habits with integrity and authenticity.

The book you hold in your hands is completely revised and expanded from the original. It's been reorganized and built on with simplicity in mind. In each chapter, you'll find a personal story from my life, followed by some discussion, Scriptures, and activities designed to engage your heart and mind. I've used various learning modalities to get you fully immersed in the reframing process. Please don't hesitate to write in this book! Write in the space I've provided and in the margins; underline to your heart's content. By the same measure, don't feel pressured to participate in a certain way. Your healing process can and should be as unique as you.

Also in each chapter you'll find a "Stepping into the Process" section with questions to get you started reframing. Any time we're learning something new or changing our direction, practice is required. By practicing new ways of living, you will eventually develop new habits that are healthy and hopeful. Don't feel compelled to answer these questions right away. Ponder them. Pray about them. Answer them bit by bit.

Finally, at the end of each chapter, I've included pages for you to journal, write questions or thoughts, or draw pictures that provide peace. Let me encourage you, though, not to limit yourself to the blank pages in this book. A journal is a great companion on the reframing journey! See your journal as *yours*; YOU get to decide how to use it. Maybe you're the type to write daily entries, poems, or pages of thoughts. Maybe you're the type to create bulleted lists or doodle or draw. Maybe you're the type to write out Scriptures, song lyrics, or quotes from others. Whomever you are, let your journal match.

To help you along the way, I've put together an acrostic. For each letter of the word *REFRAME*, I've written questions for you to ask yourself. These will help you find direction for rebuilding your life and establishing a sure foundation that will stand when life's storms come sweeping in. To make things simple, I've put the acrostic at the end of this introduction and on the bookmark included with this book.

Remember: reframing is not a step-by-step formula. It's a course of action, similar to building a new home. Your healing process is yours; you make the decisions. I'm a friend who's been there. My prayer is that this book will provide you with practical, hopeful help and that, through the hard work of reframing, you will find true, meaningful healing. God is writing your story, and reframing can be a beautiful part of it.

I would love to hear what God is doing in your life and pray alongside you as you go through this process. Please connect with me at www.reframingministries.com. You'll find articles, resources, and opportunities to engage with me and others. ***I can't wait to get to know you.***

R.E.F.R.A.M.E.

 EFLECT: What beliefs, behaviors, choices, and attitudes have brought me to where I am today?

 XAMINE: What expectations have I had of God? Am I disappointed, sad, angry, or doubting God's presence or promises?

 IND SUPPORT: Whom can I trust to walk with me through the process of mentoring and accountability?

 ENEW COMMITMENTS: Write down my values and core beliefs, and read them out loud twice a day.

 FFIRM THE POSITIVE: What goals and choices am I making for positive growth and change?

 ANAGE ADJUSTMENTS: Am I adaptable to change?

 XPLORE OPPORTUNITIES AND OPTIONS: What am I passionate about? How can God use me to help others in need?

Reframing Life

Focusing on God
When Life Gets Sideways

REVISED &
EXPANDED

Chapter One

Floating or Drowning: Reframing Time

We often feel held captive by time when, actually, it's not the clock or calendar that enslaves us . . . it's something else.

Our kayak bounced and bobbled near the buttressed, craggy cliffs of the ancient Mediterranean island. We had paddled as far as we could from the port's busy sights and sounds, then rested our oars and dangled our feet into the crystal clear waters. The tidal ebb and flow, the soft splash of waves against the coast bordered by massive boulders and volcanic rock, lulled us into rest.

And then:

Silence.

Time slowed.

The sea mist cooled our lungs . . .

Stop for a moment. Now, take one deep breath and exhale slowly.

How long has it been since you've taken time to breathe? It may be that the ebb and flow of life has become more like a surging tsunami; I understand. If you're ready to come up for air and stay up, God's life-preserver that will bring you safely to shore may be the process of *reframing* how you think about time.

Time is a gift—we didn't create it, we don't control it, and we certainly don't have a clue how long we will be confined to it here on earth. It's easy to forget that Scripture reminds us who is in charge. (*And it's* _not_ *us*—thank the Lord!)

The moment time slowed for me was during a Mediterranean cruise that I needed more than I knew! For the remainder of our trip, in the quietness of the open sea, I pondered the concept of time—especially the *present moment*, though I'm often too distracted to be aware of it. Countless times, I've missed the chance to enjoy God's presence when I needed it most because I hurried off to "fix" something He had already accomplished.

Do you struggle with being in the present too? If you feel too busy to even *consider* enjoying the moment, believe me, I get it. But: what's <u>really</u> holding you captive? We often feel held captive by time when, actually, it's not the clock or calendar that enslaves us . . . it's something else.

T.I.M.E. Inventory

As I reflected on time—its purpose, use, and how much power I give it—I asked myself some hard questions, using each letter of the word itself: *T.I.M.E.* I offer them here for you to consider SLOWLY. If you're quick to say, "Oh, of course!" or "Why, yes!" . . . Stop. Ponder. Engage. Dive in deeper.

Trust

Have I really trusted the almighty, sovereign God with my life?

1. What circumstances reveal that I trust the Lord with my <u>whole</u> life?

2. Do I worry and try to problem-solve in my own strength? How do I react to the unexpected . . . do I pray about it more than talk about it? Are my decisions driven by feelings or filtered through prayer?

3. Why am I always in a rush? Is my calendar packed with activities that leave me feeling exhausted? What do I need to cut out?

4. Proverbs 3:5–6 calls me to trust with ALL my heart. What have I not let go of? What part of my heart am I holding back?

Interests

Am I really interested in daily Christian living, or am I treating the Christian life like an emergency credit card that I pull out in a bind?

1. How much time do I spend every day cultivating a Christlike character? When something happens, do I run to Christ or someone else?

2. How much time do I spend serving others—without an agenda or expectations? Have I ever reached out to someone living with a disability, in homelessness, or in poverty? What friends, books, movies, and TV shows do I enjoy and why?

3. Colossians 3:1–4 tells us to place our minds on eternal things. Do my daily involvements reveal Christ in me? What things and thoughts have I given my mind to?

Each morning, God deposits 86,400 seconds into our bank of time. But nothing carries over to the next day. Spend it well.

—Charles R. Swindoll

 Motivation

Why do I do what I do?

1. Do I fake a smile at church on Sundays but have a different attitude through the week? Do I hold grudges? What lingering hurts or resentments might be fueling me?

2. When caregiving, do I resent having my plans interrupted? Do I help others as if I were serving Christ? When tired, do I get frustrated or run to Christ, who promises refreshment and rest (Psalm 23)?

3. Colossians 3:12–17 addresses the foundation of our motivations. How do I show love? Am I quick to judge and label, or do I step in with love? Where could I show more patience? Do my daily habits reflect the peace of Christ?

Experience

How have I responded to the experiences God has allowed?

1. When faced with trials, difficulties, and circumstances I never wanted, how do I respond? Am I holding on to bitterness? Have I honestly talked with God, sharing ALL my emotions—doubt, anger, irritation?

2. Do my doubts lead me to search the Scriptures, or am I stuck ruminating and questioning God? Do I ask, "Why?" or do I ask, "For what purpose?"

3. Paul writes in Philippians 1:29–30 about the "privilege" of suffering for Christ and doing it together. What is my response to others' suffering? What about my own? In what ways do I "rejoice with those who rejoice, and weep with those who weep" (Romans 12:15 NASB)?

Reframing Time

That is why we never give up.
Though our bodies are dying,
our spirits are being renewed every day.
For our present troubles are small
and won't last very long.
Yet they produce for us a glory
that vastly outweighs them
and will last forever!
So we don't look at the troubles
we can see now;
rather, we fix our gaze on things
that cannot be seen.
For the things we see now
will soon be gone,
but the things we cannot see
will last forever.

2 Corinthians 4:16–18

Since that sacred afternoon on the sea, I've reflected upon the T.I.M.E. model repeatedly. I've become more aware of the ways the Lord works in my life. It's my guess that you want to be more aware of His work in your life too. The good news is He's already here, willing and waiting! Are you ready to take the time to be present with Him—to be fully aware of His leading and blessing?

Stepping into the Process

- What did you spend your time doing growing up? How was time management modeled by your parents?

- What does a usual day look like for you?

- Think about your top values. Do the ways in which you spend your time reflect what you *say* you value?

- How do you *want* to use your time? What changes do you need to make?

- Do you need external support or encouragement to help you meet these goals—perhaps an app or a call from a friend?

Chapter Two

When Life Stops You in Your Tracks: Reframing Control

We often believe God is unfair, unaware, unkind, and unwilling to help when, actually, He wants to work in us through our weakness.

I came out of my mother's womb wanting to run, climb, and even fly. (Just ask her about my adventures of leaping off the fridge!) I could've been the poster child for ADHD.

ADHD has its downsides, but it has an upside too: the desire to run. As a young adult, I enjoyed many priceless mornings running with my dad. I ran several half and full marathons. When my kids were young, I kept up on a treadmill. Exercise helped me deal with episodic depression and the demanding physical duties of caregiving for a child with special needs. It released anxiety and produced positive hormones and endorphins.

Then in 2007, I became a single parent. Exercise fell off my to-do list. In 2009, I remarried (a bodybuilder, no less) and became a stepmom to two more kids. The matrix of parenting in a blended home became even more exciting . . . and much more exhausting. After two serious neck and back injuries and diagnoses of chronic fatigue or Epstein-Barr (we never found out which), arthritis, and spinal stenosis, the only things on my treadmill were layers of dust and baskets of unfolded laundry.

In 2014, my daughter's marriage engagement reignited my health regimen. "No pain, no gain!" That motto had always worked, and I had enough energy—until the day I literally couldn't get out of bed.

The doctor who saw me that afternoon ordered so many tests, the paperwork looked like a restaurant menu. The results were shocking: I had no lumbar disks. My lower vertebrae sat on top of each other like crooked bricks about to crash, pinching nerves and radiating pain throughout my body. Massive, immediate surgery was required . . . and the healing process would take up to two years.

I was *stopped* in my tracks. No warning. No clue.

Answering the Wake-up Call

It took some time, but I finally realized that, really, we're all clueless. We make our plans and lay our bricks to pave the way we want to go. We think we know what's best, but the truth is we aren't the ones best equipped to write our life stories because we cannot see what's ahead.

Often, we claim to walk by faith . . . until we're faced with the unexpected and the lights go out. There in the darkness we discover the truth about our trust in Jesus Christ. Stop and sit with this reality: **You are not in charge.** How comfortable are you with that thought? Does your faith bring you peace or are you overcome with anxiety? Do you trust that the Lord is with you even when you see no sign of His presence? These are deep, difficult questions. Letting go is an ongoing process. Where are you in it?

> *Don't try to escape pain. Pain teaches us the most important lessons.*
>
> —CHARLES R. SWINDOLL

Many of us believe we have a right to be comfortable—especially if we take extra vitamins, show a little kindness, and go to church. It's easy to believe our external behaviors measure our hearts' true condition. But then the Lord allows trials to come, and we're miffed that He didn't take notice of our neighborly kindness. When He doesn't intervene, we get fussy. After all, we planned well. We "paid it forward." Where's the little star on our life sticker chart?

Oh, my friend, I have been there! But Proverbs 16:9 reminds us:

> We can make our plans,
>> but the LORD determines our steps.

Have you ever noticed that when God instantly provides relief, we don't always recognize His grace? I believe that may be exactly why He allows our steps to include pain. Humanly, we often believe God is unfair, unaware, unkind, or unwilling to help when, actually, He wants to use our weakness to work in us. Pain may be the very thing that leads us into a deeper relationship with Him . . . and becomes a powerful way God works *through* us. Remember what Paul wrote about the thorn in his flesh?

> *Three different times I begged the Lord to take it away.*
> *Each time he said, "My grace is all you need. My power*
> *works best in weakness." So now I am glad to boast about*
> *my weaknesses, so that the power of Christ can work*
> *through me. (2 Corinthians 12:8–9)*

Jesus can use our physical infirmities and emotional wounds to help us discover where we cling to the illusion of control. He loves us extravagantly—so much so that He will stop us in our tracks and call our attention to what's best for us: Himself. Since my wake-up call of a chronic, painful diagnosis, I continually examine what matters most to me, *and I make adjustments*. Daily pain, huge scars on my stomach and back, metal disks attached to my vertebral column with metal bars and screws packed with bone from my hips—these all remind me to examine aspects of my relationship with God that I never thought about before.

Because of this, I am so thankful for the pain.

If you're ready to start reframing control, I have a challenge for you: schedule one to two hours to be alone in your favorite, quiet place—perhaps in a chair on your patio, under a tree at the park, or in the courtyard at your church. For me, it's by a quiet stream or gentle waterfall. (I've had seasons where it was in my small closet!) The best place is one you choose, free of as many distractions as possible.

Take this book, a Bible, a pair of earbuds, and whatever you use to listen to music. When you arrive, first listen to worshipful music and read Psalm 23. When you're ready, consider the questions below.

1. Has God allowed you to walk through a "valley of the shadow of death"? Perhaps a failed marriage, a disabled parent or child, a betrayal, or an infirmity? Examine that challenge and how you have—or have not—embraced it.

2. Are you willing to believe that God has allowed your circumstance because He loves you and is calling you to a deeper relationship with Him?

3. Are you willing to give up what you want and accept what He has allowed?

4. Have you taken comfort in the Shepherd's "rod and staff"?

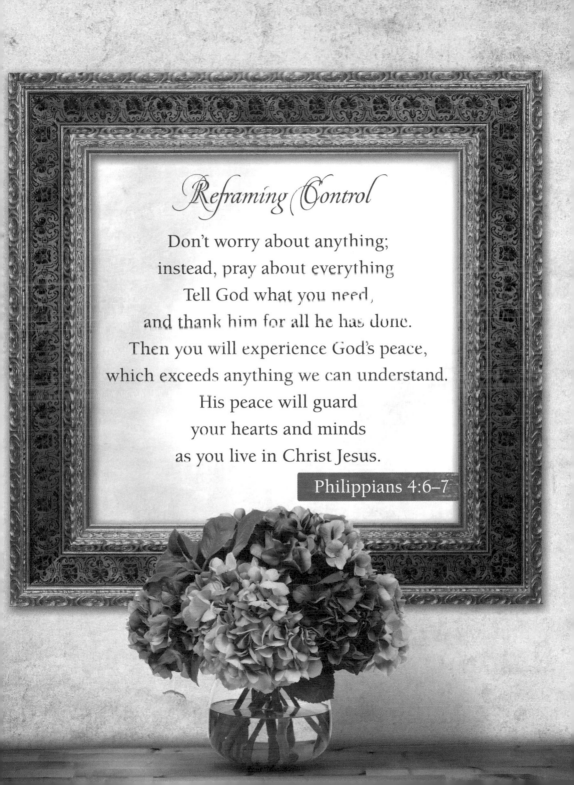

Reframing Control

Don't worry about anything;
instead, pray about everything
Tell God what you need,
and thank him for all he has done.
Then you will experience God's peace,
which exceeds anything we can understand.
His peace will guard
your hearts and minds
as you live in Christ Jesus.

Philippians 4:6–7

The Enemy loves for us to believe we can control our lives. Certainly, we are to be responsible! But responsibility and control are vastly different. Control is self-focused; responsibility is God (and others)-focused. To keep my control instincts in check, I ask myself daily, *Am I allowing God to be on His throne? If not, what do I need to release?*

The Great Physician takes what is broken in us and creates something beautiful. But until you allow Him to have full control, you <u>will</u> experience inner conflict. Having been on both sides, I will tell you that giving God center place will bring you unimaginable freedom and joy—whatever your circumstances.

Stepping into the Process

- How was control handled in your childhood home? Did your parents hold tightly to the reigns, or did you see them looking to God for direction?

- Has control ever been inappropriately used against you? How have those experiences shaped your approach to control today?

- When you make plans, do you ask for the Lord's direction, or do you start praying *after* you've jumped in?

- What will you do to find support in the ongoing process of relying on Jesus? Is there a group at your church? A counselor? A weekly coffee date with a friend?

Chapter Three

Flying Fish with Party Straws: Reframing Your Mind-set

*Joy, peace, hope, perseverance, endurance, unity,
love, grace, mercy, and so much more
are cultivated by what we feed our minds.*

T wo days after massive back surgery, I was in a hospital bed, hooked up to a pump primed with enough morphine to kill pain at a level that would make childbirth feel like a bellyache. My loving husband had taken off two weeks to set up camp under my hospital room's third-story window. Spring storms pounded Dallas. Water drops danced in the wind, refracting light like fireworks.

My husband had drifted off to sleep when I glanced over and saw something through the window—something moving, or rather, softly floating: sparkling, blue fish with party straws in their mouths. (You read that right.)

Staring, I thought, *Raindrops drip. They don't float. They don't look like fish, and even if they did, fish don't use party straws.* Not wanting to wake my weary husband (or sound like a freak), I stayed quiet.

Two days passed. I snuck peeks to see if my floating friends were still alive and well. They were. What's more, they were growing in number and variety. Joining the sparkly, blue fish were long-legged, skinny-looking spiders—a little parade floating right outside my window!

Still, I said nothing, not even when the little creatures entered my hospital bathroom, walking impressively in single file on the grout lines like preschoolers holding a rope on a field trip. But then things got even weirder. Along with the fish and spider parade, bubbles of all sizes began appearing on the bathroom floor.

I lost it.

Perched on the toilet with my feet suspended, I yelled for my husband. "Just look at the hordes of bugs and bubbles!!" I squealed when he hurried in. His silence and tilted head spoke volumes. Finally, he answered: "Um, Sweetie, the floor is clean and dry. I'm not sure what you're seeing."

"Not sure? They're *everywhere*, Honey! Spiders, bubbles, look!"

Another long pause . . . then his tone softened like he was talking a skittish cat out of a tree. "You're gonna be okay," he said. "Let's talk about it more when you're back in bed."

I Can See Clearly Now

Turns out I'm allergic to most painkillers. They make me hallucinate (obviously!). I get a little delusional and paranoid. I get itchy and really cranky. When we realized the bubbles, spiders, and flying fish were manifestations of drug allergies, I quit taking the culprit . . . and the hallucinations disappeared. My relief outweighed the increased physical pain and muscle spasms. A clear mind means everything to me.

Never take for granted the fact that we have God's mind in writing. It's called the Bible.

—CHARLES R. SWINDOLL

Paul spoke repeatedly of the importance of consistently guarding our minds with truth. To the church in Rome he wrote: "Don't copy the behavior and customs of this world, but let God transform you into a new person by changing the way you think" (Romans 12:2). To the believers in Colossae, he penned: "Think about the things of heaven, not the things of earth (Colossians 3:2). To his friends in Philippi, he urged: "Fix your thoughts on what is true, and honorable, and right, and pure, and lovely, and admirable. Think about things that are excellent and worthy of praise" (Philippians 4:8).

Why would God direct Paul to spend so many words addressing our minds? Because our minds direct what we believe! Our perspectives form in our minds . . . and from our perspectives flow our behaviors. The mind keeps our imaginations, affections, and passions in check. Joy, peace, hope, perseverance, endurance, unity, love, grace, mercy, and so much more are cultivated by what we feed our minds. Our character and integrity rest upon our mind-sets.

God tells us to guard our minds with His truth because otherwise our minds will conjure up things much worse than spider parades and fish parties! Remember in Judges when "all the people did whatever seemed right in their own eyes" (Judges 17:6)? What "seemed right" brought Israel years of enemy occupation, wars, famine, abuse, and murder . . . and our minds aren't any better than theirs! Thankfully, God has a clear mind and is available to us always. We don't have to do whatever seems right to us; we can *know* what's right. We can reframe our mind-sets according to God's Word.

The Bible may not include the word *reframe*, but it certainly includes all the principles we need to do it. The following four Es will help you in the ongoing process of reframing your mind-set. As you read them, write a few practical notes about how you will put each into practice in your daily life. <u>Be specific</u>.

1. *Establish* **your foundation on God's Word to find joy, peace, and insight.**

> *The commandments of the Lord are right,*
> *bringing joy to the heart.*
> *The commandments of the Lord are clear,*
> *giving insight for living*
> (Psalm 19:8)

2. *Enrich* **your mind with truth for steadfast strength and life.**

> *Your eternal word, O Lord,*
> *stands firm in heaven.*
> *Your faithfulness extends to every generation,*
> *as enduring as the earth you created.*
> *Your regulations remain true to this day,*
> *for everything serves your plans.*
> *If your instructions hadn't sustained me with joy,*
> *I would have died in my misery.*
> *I will never forget your commandments,*
> *for by them you give me life.*
> (Psalm 119:89–93)

3. *Encourage* one another to cultivate unity.

> *Don't use foul or abusive language.*
> *Let everything you say be good and helpful, so that*
> *your words*
> *will be an encouragement to those who hear them.*
> (Ephesians 4:29)

4. *Examine* your heart consistently to be a person of integrity.

> *Declare me innocent, O LORD,*
> *for I have acted with integrity;*
> *I have trusted in the LORD without wavering.*
> *Put me on trial, LORD, and cross-examine me.*
> *Test my motives and my heart.*
> (Psalm 26:1–2)

Few things make you realize the value of a solid mind-set like hallucinations! Seeing things that were not really there floating through the air and marching across the floor was incredibly disconcerting. It made me realize the necessity of caring for and keeping control of our minds . . . and that's central to the reframing process!

Reframing Your Mind-set

Letting your sinful nature control your mind
leads to death.
But letting the Spirit control your mind
leads to life and peace.

Romans 8:6

Remember: Reframing means choosing to incorporate a different perspective than the one we come by naturally. It means taking a step back and considering the frame through which we see reality. When you reframe, you say, "Let's look at this situation another way." I'm living proof that you can come at something countless ways, but until you come at it through the lens of God's truth, you will be disappointed.

Reframing doesn't mean your circumstances change, your pain disappears, or the life you planned happens. It means you have the clarity to grow and thrive regardless of those circumstances. And no matter the issue, the reframing process begins and ends with your mind-set. Only God's truth can help us see life clearly. Without it, the floors will bubble up in no time!

Stepping into the Process

- How are you protecting your mind? What activities do you do to keep your mind actively connected to the Lord instead of being pulled into the day's distractions?

- How do you handle your emotions? Are they harnessed, or do you allow them to take over?

- Are you actively hiding God's Word in your heart?

- Have you invited the Lord to examine your soul?

- Do you have a few close friends who speak truth into your life—friends who hold you accountable for how you're using your mind?

Notes

Chapter Four

Beauty Unimagined:
Reframing Dead Ends

Stop chasing illusions and go the way of God—
who created you, knows you,
and is longing to lead you to the fullest life.

A few years ago, I nearly incinerated my finger with a hot glue gun. I was working on a project for my daughter Ashley's wedding and almost welded my finger to the table. While I soaked my scalded hand in ice, with the other, I dusted off her baby photo albums.

One turn of a page and I was swept back in time. Her sassy smile, blonde curls, little round face, and blue eyes almost looked through me. The button-trimmed, pristine pages lined with pink presented the illusion that I could keep her life—*our lives*—from being flawed and damaged. The sun set, my finger cooled, and the visual reminders of days gone by sunk deep into my soul.

As the years passed in those albums, the photos of Ashley revealed subtle changes. Her smile wasn't as wide. Her eyes that once danced with delight had become dull and distant. Her animated enthusiasm had turned inward. Two younger siblings—one with an unbelievable amount of needs, many moves from house to house, and my pursuit of having the "perfect" family had obviously taken a toll on her life. In those days, I did what most do when they believe in illusions: I worked harder at doing the same things . . . and I ended up further down the wrong road.

Believe me. Staying on the wrong road never works out well. When we use more force to keep moving in the wrong direction, we eventually hit dead ends. I know because I plowed right into some big ones.

Turning Around

Sometimes coming to the end of the road is the best thing that can happen in our lives because it forces us to turn in the direction God wants us to go. At first, we hate that we have to turn around. We blame God for not holding up His end of the deal (whatever that "deal" was). We feel helpless and hopeless and lost. Then, when we see that we made a "God-sized" wrong turn and that only God's way is the right way . . . we finally, *gratefully*, let Him lead.

On occasion, we reach that dead end, come to the realization we're not getting through it no matter how hard we try, and hightail it the other direction. Most often, though, the turnaround goes slowly . . . and that's by design. Healing—from wounds we've endured or inflicted on ourselves—takes time.

For me, finally letting God lead took me to a slow-moving road I like to call Route 5 (a.m.). It began when Ashley was a teenager. The Lord prompted me to spend special, focused time with just her. But the only time of day I could do it was before my son with disabilities woke up—before 6:00 a.m. She agreed to wake up with me at 5:00 in the morning.

This was huge! My daughter and I are <u>not</u> morning people. I could hardly believe she had agreed to this idea that, frankly, sounded nuts even to me. When the Lord first brought it to mind, my know-it-all thought was, *How can anything be done when we're too tired to talk?* My old parenting route had included a lot of talking . . . and very little relationship. God's new path inherently changed up at least one element of that equation. I could barely think, much less talk that early, which is EXACTLY what my daughter needed: a mother who would shut up and LISTEN. You see, when God moves mountains, the route we're used to turns to rubble—often to create a roadblock that forces us to let Him lead us to a new path we would've never considered on our own. It made no sense to me then, but God knew 5 a.m. was exactly what we needed.

So, we did it. We got up. We met in the living room in our PJs. I planned NOTHING for our time together—no devotional or prayer, no Scripture-memory program or Bible study. I planned only one thing: to be with my daughter and to listen. Most of the time, we sat by the fireplace, and then we fell back to sleep after about fifteen minutes. But to this day, she says that God started His renovation work in her life when she and I spent that predawn time together. In the quiet, something miraculous began to happen. It always does when we stop talking and start listening.

November 2014, Ashley was married—almost twenty-two years to the day after she was born. As I watched her walk down the aisle, I could see that the sparkle in her eyes had returned. Her wedding veil was lifted by the love of her life . . . almost as gently as God's light lifts the veil of darkness when we finally take the path He directs. But *we* must step down that aisle with surrender, humility, confession, and a quiet confidence that what He has started will be fully completed— perfectly crafted by His hands.

You can have peace and a new direction in life. How?
Receive the forgiveness Jesus Christ offers you.

—CHARLES R. SWINDOLL

Paul wrote of that confidence to the church at Philippi: "And I am certain that God, who began the good work within you, will continue his work until it is finally finished on the day when Christ Jesus returns" (Philippians 1:6). Christ doesn't tell us HOW He will work things out or what He's up to in the process. It isn't our right to know; it's our call to trust. The first step toward significant change always demands we trust in what we cannot yet see.

If you belong to Jesus, that promise in Philippians is yours. I encourage you to write, here or in your journal, about the good work that God began in you on the day you said "Yes!" to new life in Jesus Christ. When was it? Where were you? What sounds did you hear? What scents drifted through the air? Get yourself back to that place and think of where you were before Jesus and where you are today. Now ask yourself, *Am I willing to go wherever He takes me?*

For some of you, this is a wake-up call. That dead end isn't far ahead. *Stop chasing illusions and go the way of God—who created you, knows you, and is longing to lead you to the fullest life.* For others, it's a flag unfolding on that wall you've slammed into: "God is right behind you." The One who loves you most is ready to help you live with hope and joy; don't delay! And for others, it's a reminder that walking with God—though never a dead end—is not always a perfectly laid-out picture-book page. It helps to reframe the "straight and narrow" as one of life's grand adventures, which always includes some twists and turns you never expected. When you stop fighting for control, you'll be free to enjoy every part of the journey.

Reframing Dead Ends

We also pray that you will be
strengthened with all his glorious
power
so you will have all the endurance
and patience you need.
May you be filled with joy,
always thanking the Father.
He has enabled you to share in the
inheritance that belongs to
his people,
who live in the light.
For he has rescued us from
the kingdom of darkness
and transferred us into
the Kingdom of his dear Son,
who purchased our freedom
and forgave our sins.

Colossians 1:11–14

Remember: When we hit dead ends, we must develop new habits, which come from making better choices day by day. Is it time to reflect on what has led you to where you are today? The Lord alone can guide you from self-destruction to beauty unimagined.

Stepping into the Process

- What were your motivations behind the decisions that led you to the place you are today?

- Have you ever outlined your values? Have you written out your commitment to stick to them?

- What options do you have in taking a new direction?

- What direction do you believe is <u>God's</u> direction? What evidence leads you to this conclusion?

Notes

Chapter Five

Tired of Being Disappointed? Reframing Your Expectations

Maybe God is calling you to examine your expectations, to align your will with His—based on His Word —instead of demanding He align with your plan.

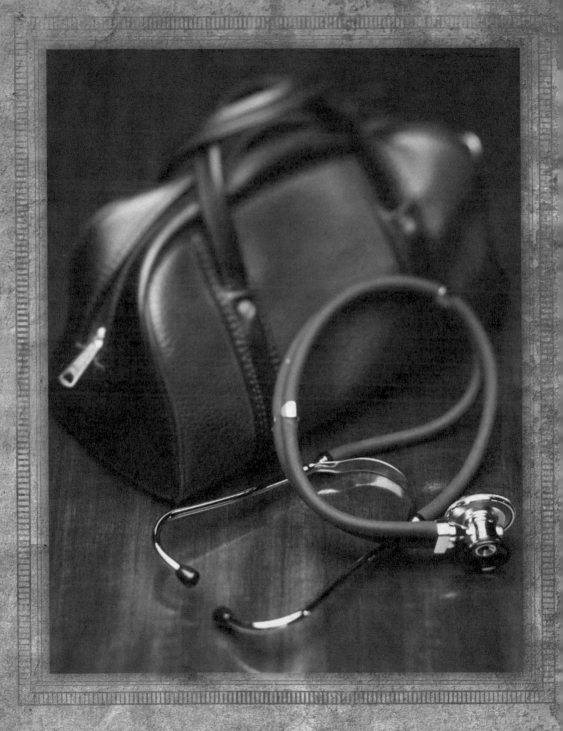

A few years ago, I asked my son Austin to come with us on the Insight for Living Ministries Alaska Cruise Conference to help us look after my other son with special needs, Jon. With many speaking and book engagements, I planned for Austin to help while I worked—a win-win because Jon loves spending time with his older brother. They have a tried-and-true, tremendously tender sibling relationship. Austin arrived home from his university at the end of June, and we set sail. As expected, Jon was delighted!

What we *didn't* expect was for Austin to get terribly sick—so sick that he wasn't able to return to his university apartment until the end of July. Years ago, I would've considered such an illness a frustration, but age and time have a way of teaching us what's important. I viewed our extra month together as a gift. Our discussions and laughter deepened our relationship. We talked about *everything*. We pondered the future and expressed our hopes.

I don't know how life will unfold for Austin . . . or for any of my kids . . . or for you and me. I do know that regardless of what unfolds, we CAN enjoy life fully *IF* we align ourselves with God's sovereign will. Notice I didn't say we can be fully *happy*; I said, "we can enjoy life fully." That comes down to one key ingredient: *attitude*.

Throughout July, Austin couldn't control his sickness . . . but he could control his attitude. We planned for an amazing cruise. We experienced a beautiful one, amid illness, because we *chose* to find the beauty in it. Austin had planned on enjoying a summer with his university friends and earning money. Instead, his illness cost him his job, but we had a meaningful, quiet month together at home because we chose not to be shaken by interruptions to our plans.

Sometimes it's that easy; other times it's excruciatingly difficult.

Asking Yourself the Hardest Questions

Have you ever expected one thing only to find God allowed something else? How did you respond? As you sorted through your disappointment, did you think about what your expectations were?

1. What are/were your expectations? Of God? Yourself? Your spouse? Your family? Your job? Your church? Write out your answers . . . **and be honest**. Don't write the answers you know you should; write the ones you know are true.

2. Now assess your expectations of people, things, and circumstances according to Scripture. What does God's Word say about each? For some, you may already know exactly what the Bible says;

for others, you'll need to do some digging. Take the time! Use the chart below to help you organize your thoughts.

My Expectation of . . .	What Scripture Says

If you're like me, you didn't score a 100 on your expectation list. Our expectations are often rooted in creature comforts—relief rather than resilience, human peace rather than eternal perseverance, recognition rather than respect for God. Psalm 37 calls us to trust in God, commit our ways to Him, be still, and release our worry. When we choose to place God first and focus fully on honoring, loving, and obeying Him, the desires of our hearts change. We care more about developing Christlike character than gaining temporary, earthly comfort. <u>Getting to the ROOT of our expectations changes everything</u>.

As you learn to reframe your expectations with God's Word, you'll see them shift from being self-focused to God-focused. His truth will help you choose to be more aware, attentive, and alive in your current circumstances. You'll begin to see where God is at work and to expect that He will use *every* experience in your life to bring Him glory and honor!

3. Take some time now to ponder how He has worked in and through you when you were most disappointed.

My Desires and Expectations	God's Work in Me When I Am Disappointed

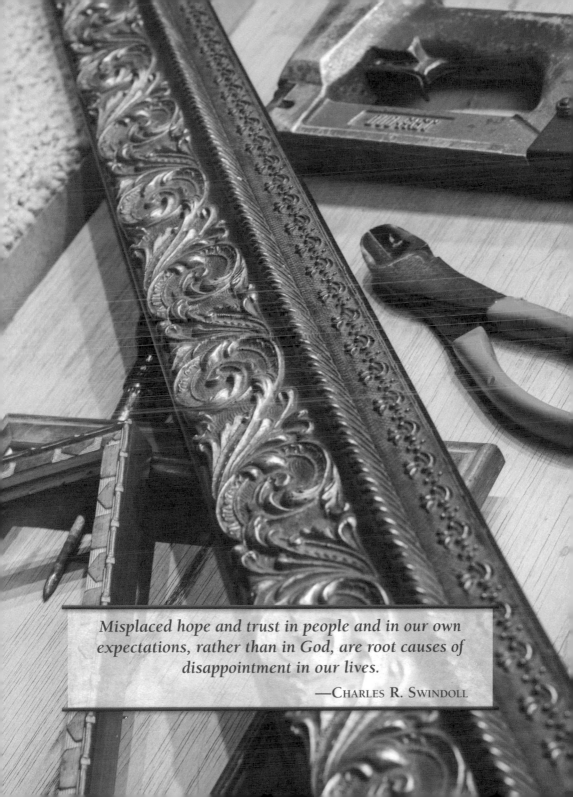

Misplaced hope and trust in people and in our own expectations, rather than in God, are root causes of disappointment in our lives.

—CHARLES R. SWINDOLL

July ended, and Austin's health returned. As he headed back to school, my tears dripped and I reminded myself that God is in control . . . of Austin's life and of mine. I felt quiet contentment as I watched his car turn the corner and disappear. The previous month didn't go at all as planned. In another stage of life, it would've been a frustrating, fruitless disaster. But because Austin and I have each taken time to work on reframing our expectations and attitudes, when things went awry, we got something much better than we ever could've planned.

Reframing my expectations is a <u>constant</u> process. Sometimes I succeed. When I don't, I take heart that I'm not alone. Even John the Baptizer, the one God chose to announce the coming Messiah, struggled with expectations. Read Matthew 11. What happened in verses 2 and 3?

> *John the Baptist, who was in prison, heard about all the things the Messiah was doing. So he sent his disciples to ask Jesus, "Are you the Messiah we've been expecting, or should we keep looking for someone else?"* (Matthew 11:2–3)

Things weren't going the way John thought they would. His faithfulness had landed him in prison. The Messiah was taking His sweet time. John began to doubt his own message.

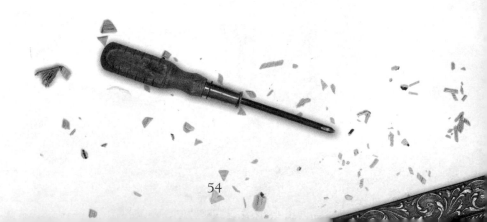

The word Jesus sent back to John overflowed with graceful assurance: Tell him all the miracles you've witnessed (all the expectations you've seen turned upside down). Tell him, "'God blesses those who do not fall away because of me'" (Matthew 11:6). The Lord went on to address John's disciples. Whom had they expected to find in the wilderness? Certainly not a "mad" man sporting camel-hair duds and chomping on locusts and honey! But look what Jesus said of John, the one who just moments before had doubted Jesus: "'I tell you the truth, of all who have ever lived, none is greater than John the Baptist'" (11:11).

My friend, I don't know where you find yourself today: saying goodbye, battling disappointments, receiving unexpected news, wrestling with the betrayal of an unfaithful spouse, or reeling from the sting of a legalistic church—I don't know. But I *do* know nothing surprises our Lord. He *is* good despite what we perceive as bad. He's good despite what IS bad!

Sometimes what we see as God's "absence" is actually His waiting patiently for us to draw near. I won't pretend to know what God has in mind for you, but I do know He cares. I also know that Jesus was willing to disappoint everyone, except for the Father. Why? Because He loves us—too much to let us sacrifice His best for our lesser expectations! The Lord constantly works to transform our childish faith into one of mature substance. Often, that means we experience momentary disappointments that can shift our attention from creature comforts to the Creator Himself. As our expectations become more biblical, so do our attitudes, so we'll be ready to handle the unexpected with grace.

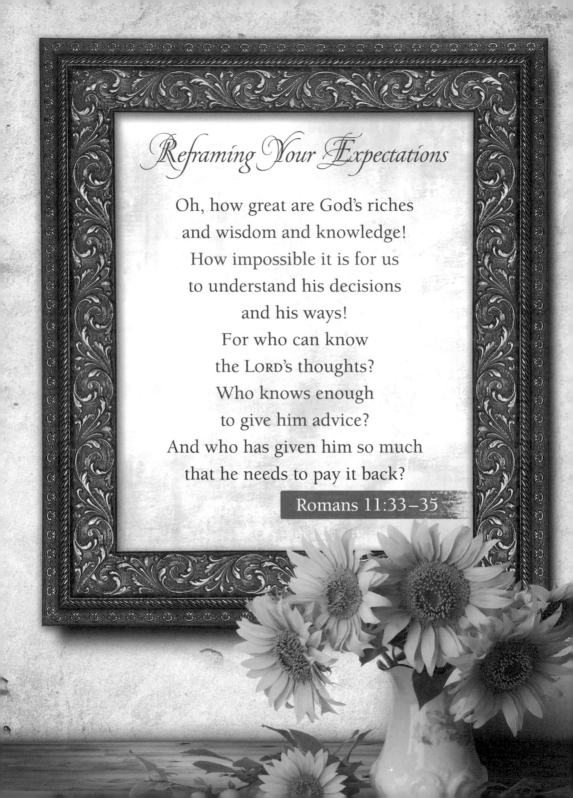

Reframing Your Expectations

Oh, how great are God's riches
and wisdom and knowledge!
How impossible it is for us
to understand his decisions
and his ways!
For who can know
the LORD's thoughts?
Who knows enough
to give him advice?
And who has given him so much
that he needs to pay it back?

Romans 11:33–35

Are you tired of being disappointed? Maybe God is calling you to examine your expectations, to align your will with His—based on His Word—instead of demanding He align with *your* plan. It's amazing what can happen when we admit our failed expectations, embrace our circumstances, and ask God to direct our attitudes and steps. The road still won't be easy, but you'll travel with far fewer frustrations and far more peace.

Stepping into the Process

- Are you continually frustrated, feeling like God has let you down? What does that tell you about your expectations?

- Have you looked for what is possible in what appears impossible? What did you find?

- Are you around people and in places now that you never would've been if the unexpected hadn't happened?

- How can you use what you never expected to bring honor and glory to God?

- How can God use your life to connect with others in ways you never anticipated?

Chapter Six

As Easy as "Cheese!" Reframing Influence

*You have influence! Your influence is powerful!
And your influence can change lives
everywhere you go.*

My husband and I both went through painful divorces before we met each other. Not so long ago, he shared something with me from that difficult season of his life. He said he FORCED himself to smile every day, even though he felt rotten.

He made it a habit to smile *everywhere*. He smiled in the shower. He smiled when he looked in the mirror getting ready for the day. He smiled as he drove to work. He smiled when he passed the mail carrier, when he checked out of the grocery store, when he sat at a stoplight, when a stranger walked by the front yard, when he caught his reflection in a window. He smiled as often as he could through those awful, long, difficult days.

Want to know what I love about him more than just about anything else? His incredible positivity and his willingness to offer every single person a smile, no matter what. On my very worst days, he influences me in a most powerful way.

Our society has lost track of what influence really is. We believe having influence means having a big audience, attending a huge church, knowing popular people, holding countless degrees, owning lots of stuff, or having big bank accounts. But those who have had the most influence on my life have never ultimately been known for their riches, their reach, or their social recognition. They are known, above all else, for their character.

Think about the people of upstanding character you know. I'm willing to bet they all have at least one thing in common—a powerful yet personal life perspective. That perspective allows them to be at peace with this life . . . and it shows on their faces.

The Face of Influence

A few years ago, I attended a conference where one of the speakers touched on the subject of influence. Honestly, I had rarely considered myself a person with much influence . . . until I heard this speaker's talk.

It's my assumption that many of you reading these words believe you have little influence too. But you'd be surprised. Of the speaker's ten points, one was so simple. Yet it completely changed my perception of influence. Are you ready for it?

Smiling!

That's it! Really! We are "wonderfully complex" (Psalm 139:14), created with marvelous workmanship by a loving God to connect with one another without saying a word. All you have to do is give away a simple smile, and ta-da! You've just influenced someone's life. That person may never tell you, but I WILL: one smile can be a game changer.

When I left the conference, I couldn't get this idea out of my mind, so I jotted down some notes about smiling based on my experience and research:[1]

- **Smiling is attractive!** In 2011, the Face Research Laboratory at the University of Aberdeen, Scotland, performed a study to evaluate the relationship between smiling and attractiveness. The results? Both men and women are more attracted to those who make eye contact and smile than to those who do not.

- **Smiling—like yawning—is very contagious.** In 2003, researchers in Sweden found that the cingulate cortex—an unconscious automatic response area of the brain—is responsible for our happy facial expressions, even if we're simply mimicking someone else's smile. In other words, when presented with a smiling face, it takes conscious effort to turn your own smile upside down!

- **Smiling improves our moods and physical well-being.** When you smile, your brain releases endorphins, dopamine, and serotonin, simultaneously boosting your mood, relaxing your body, and improving your heart function. When you smile at someone, you create a symbiotic relationship that allows both of you to release those feel-good chemicals, making you both more attractive and increasing the chances that you will both live longer, healthier lives!

My experience of raising a neurologically challenged son has given me plenty of opportunity to see that last point in action. We've

The joy of touching other people's lives is the greatest adventure in the family of God.

—Charles R. Swindoll

practiced smiling so many times at our house, I can testify beyond a doubt to its positive effect. When our smiles turn into laughter, the endorphin levels soar—and believe me, that makes you feel better no matter what kind of shape you're in!

Several years ago, I was in a car accident that caused me serious head and face trauma. I couldn't get out of bed, so my kids would bring their laptops onto my bed and show me hilarious videos. Because of the broken bones in my face, I had to be careful not to laugh *too* hard, but smiling and laughing lifted my mood more than I can say.

My kids influenced me with their smiles, just as my husband does! And think of this: in both cases, their smiles had a positive impact on them too. Laughing with me helped my kids get through the after-shocks of a loved one being in a terrible accident. It counteracted fear and smothered the frustration of not having Mom do as much as she normally does. Smiling got my husband through his painful divorce. (Is there any other kind?) Smiling forced him to shift his focus from everything in his life that made him feel miserable onto the good gifts he did have.

What does that tell me? Influence starts within. And it's something we *all* have—including YOU. You have influence! Your influence is powerful! And your influence can change lives everywhere you go.

If you want to have a proper perspective, be a person of character, and use your influence for good, it will take hard work, patience, and a lot of grace. But it can start with something simple. So, turn up the corners of your mouth and give away a warm smile!

Need a little help finding something to smile about? My dad has some advice: read Psalm 103:1–6 out loud. (Reading out loud is a powerful reinforcer!)

> *Let all that I am praise the Lord;*
>> *with my whole heart, I will praise his holy name.*
>
> *Let all that I am praise the Lord;*
>> *may I never forget the good things he does for me.*
>
> *He forgives all my sins*
>> *and heals all my diseases.*
>
> *He redeems me from death*
>> *and crowns me with love and tender mercies.*
>
> *He fills my life with good things.*
>> *My youth is renewed like the eagle's!*
>
> *The Lord gives righteousness*
>> *and justice to all who are treated unfairly.*

Have you counted the good gifts the Father of Lights has given you—forgiveness, redemption, love, mercy, tenderness, righteousness? Take the time to write out the things in your life that you have never thought of as gifts, and express your gratitude for them.

Gift	Gratitude

Reframing Influence

A cheerful look
brings joy to the heart;
good news makes for good health.

Proverbs 15:30

Cultivating gratitude in your life will change your perspective, making it easier to show off your toothy grin. As you do, I promise—you'll feel better, *and* you'll have some incredible stories to share.

Stepping into the Process

- When you were growing up, did people in your home smile and laugh?

- Are you embarrassed or afraid to give away a smile? If so, why?

- How has a smile—given or received—changed your day?

- How can you incorporate your beautiful smile into a life-giving opportunity for you and others?

Notes

Chapter Seven

Where Character Blooms: Reframing Loneliness

Being alone may be the very place where God wants to speak to us— without the clatter that so invades our cluttered lives.

The groundskeeper and his young wife had just moved to Dallas. He was a new student entering seminary on probation. The school grounds he tended were manicured to perfection. Bright flowers and freshly cut grass looked like gift-wrapped packages welcoming incoming students. It was a blistering-hot August. Sweat burned his eyes. Wiping his brow, he couldn't help but think back to those long, lonely months serving overseas with the U.S. Marine Corps . . .

Just a few years into marriage, the letter had arrived, calling him to a tour of duty on the other side of the world. He kissed his bride goodbye and set sail for Okinawa, not knowing another soul on board. As the seas rolled by, the ship plunged into a massive storm. He pulled from his bag Elisabeth Elliot's book *Through Gates of Splendor* and sat on the stone-cold deck fighting seasickness. Smothered in lonely sorrow with nothing but time, he examined his soul.

In Okinawa, women of ill repute lined the streets. Overcome with desire and the dark deception of sexual temptation, many of his fellow Marines ran into their alluring arms. But this young Marine resisted. In fact, while on that island, he connected with a Christian mentor who told him to run—literally *run*—past them. And he did! After eighteen months away, the future groundskeeper ran back into his wife's arms—a pure man who had never succumbed to the seductions of the beautiful women on that lonely island.

His time away was <u>thoroughly</u> life-changing. The young Marine had planned to return and work in a machine shop. But God had other plans. By putting the young man alone on an island of temptations, away from everything familiar and comfortable, God tested his character. As he clung to Christ, the Marine's heart was transformed . . . so much so that when he returned to the States, he and his young bride dedicated their entire lives to pursuing a new direction: full-time ministry.

Right away, he enrolled in Dallas Theological Seminary—and was scared to death because he did not have an appropriate college degree. With only his wife's income as a bank secretary, and with no other resources, he worked as the groundskeeper to make ends meet. This gave him lots of opportunities to sit on a garden bench with his new professor and mentor, Christian Education Professor Howard Hendricks. Dr. Hendricks, always encouraging, believed in this "on probation" student before he believed in himself, and that finally gave the student the confidence he needed by his third year to believe he really could do the work. When graduation day arrived, he received three of the seminary's highest honors: the Harry A. Ironside Award in Expository Preaching, the Faculty Award for the Best All-Around Student, and The Christian Education Award, the top award in the field of his major.

Stepping Stones That Lead to a Beautiful Garden

Have you guessed the name of that young Marine? Chuck Swindoll, *my dad.*

It was my dad who ran past those women and didn't compromise his wedding vows. It was my dad who pushed a mower and trimmed hedges in the Texas heat as a groundskeeper. It was my dad who entered Dallas Theological Seminary on probation and graduated with highest honors. And it *is* my dad who for more than six decades has taught truth and grace to countless people.

My dad's discipline of character didn't begin on that ship headed for Okinawa. It may have entered the crucible then, but it began years before—when he was a boy, singing with my Aunt Luci and Uncle Orville at the soda shop to earn ice cream cones . . . without a penny in their pockets. It shone as a young husband when he helped my mom through deep, dark depression while raising two kids—a 26-month-old son and a 3-month-old daughter. It shown as I grew up, when he and Mom started Insight for Living Ministries. Since he was a full-time pastor, he asked Mom to lead that ministry. In order for their parental responsibilities to be appropriately accomplished, he helped Mom teach us how to do laundry. They shared driving us to and from school. He even planted his own gardens. It continued to shine into my adulthood when he and Mom helped my sister and me through divorces, occasionally took his grandkids to school, and lingered in waiting rooms as doctors tried to fix the chronic pain my mother, sister, and I suffer from.

My dad's character shines as brightly as it does because he *daily* chooses to surrender his life and say yes to God without compromise. And though he may be years and miles from Okinawa, my dad makes time every single day to be alone with God, sowing the Word into his heart.

My dad's life gives testimony to two truths: First, character isn't cultivated quickly. It's developed one decision after another over time . . . a long, long time. Each choice is like a stepping stone along the long path of life. Some are smooth and simple; making the leap to them is easy because we can see the path in front of us. It's a different story when we can't see our hands in front of our faces, much less the other side of the stone. Those rough stones shrouded by clouds of loneliness, desire, and fear—those are the ones that significantly change our lives. Each step requires deeper trust that our Shepherd is good and able.

He will make us "surefooted as a deer, able to tread upon the heights" (Habakkuk 3:19). His Word will light our path as we step out on what feels like the very edge of a cliff (Psalm 119:105).

We cling; He carries . . . one single step at a time.

Second, my dad's life shows that character is often refined and maintained when we're alone—either literally or in situations that overwhelm us with loneliness. Many of us run *from* loneliness and silence, and we run *to* distractions. We think if we're alone, something must be wrong . . . when, actually, being alone may be the very place where God wants to speak to us—without the clatter that so invades our cluttered lives. In lonely circumstances, our responses reveal the truth about what we believe. And it's often when we are all alone that we make life's most powerful choices.

1. Think about someone you respect, whose character you would like to emulate. How have times alone contributed to his or her character? If you don't know, I challenge you to ask that person. Then take a few moments to write down key points from his or her story.

2. Now, think about your own story. How have times of loneliness shaped your character? What fruit do you see from them? What lessons have you learned? How have you used them to positively impact others? *How could you?*

Character is the moral and spiritual undergirding that reinforces a life and that resists the temptation to compromise.

—CHARLES R. SWINDOLL

Reframing Loneliness

How can a young person stay pure?
By obeying your word.
I have tried hard to find you—
don't let me wander
from your commands.
I have hidden your word
in my heart,
that I might not sin against you.

Psalm 119:9–11

Sometimes God pulls us out of everything we planned in order to prepare us for purposes we never imagined. Someday, you may be all alone on a bunk bed or office chair . . . business trip or Internet chatroom . . . empty nest or funeral parlor. Temptation will cross your path. In those moments, your choices could change your life . . . and the lives of countless others. What choices will you make then? What choices will you make today?

Remember: Every step matters, whether it's on the mountaintop or in the valley. So keep stepping out with faith and clinging to the Shepherd. He's got you!

Stepping into the Process

- Are you spending time *alone* sowing God's Word into your heart, *daily* planting its guidelines and truths deep into your soul?

- Have you considered how moments, months, or years of solitude might be sacred?

- Are you running toward temporary seductions that promise earthly relief, or are you running toward a truly authentic relationship with Christ?

- Is there a "stone" ahead of you that you cannot see? What do you need to do to step out in faith?

Chapter Eight

Seizing Life's Shocking Surprises: Reframing Crises

You and I are spiritual athletes. We're faced with insurmountable odds that challenge us to either resort to being spiritual couch potatoes or to endure our training with Christ.

My son Jon let out a yell. Chairs tumbled over. His cell phone slid across the wood floor.

By the time I reached him, the grand mal seizure had started. Without warning, Jon's body was bombarded by electrical and chemical blasts that slammed him like tidal waves.

Let's be clear: I'm not the "stay-calm-during-a-seizure" sort of person. That's like saying, "Stay calm," to passengers on an airplane nosediving directly toward earth. Not gonna happen. Instead, I did what has become second nature to those of us who live in the insanely unpredictable space named "Seizure Disorders": I yelled for my husband, kicked over the chair before Jon's head hit it again, turned him on his side to allow saliva and blood to drain out of his mouth, held his shaking head, and waited.

Although seizures often last less than a minute, it feels like Christ will return before they end. And there's *nothing* to do but wait them out and keep the seizing person safe. After each seizure, Jon's memory is short-circuited—often for days—and he's left wondering what on earth happened. He asks repeatedly: "Why do I have seizures?" "Why do they hurt me?" "When will my pain go away?"

Between his questions, I cancel meetings, prepare calming baths, give medicine, make doctor appointments, and offer my opinion to the Lord about how seizures are totally unnecessary and should be removed from earth.

You may or may not have experienced a seizure, but undoubtedly life has thrown you into unexpected, painful circumstances. When we're seized by the unexpected, the same emotions surface in most of us. We start out feeling shocked. We go numb, fall to the ground, flounder, and wonder how something so excruciating could happen. We shake our fists at the heavens and ask repeatedly: "Why did this have to happen?" "When will it be over?" "Lord, **where are you?**"

A Golden Opportunity

Have you ever considered that in the middle of our physical, emotional, spiritual, and financial crises, the Lord drops a golden opportunity into our laps? Granted, it's an opportunity no one wants, but it's priceless just the same: **the opportunity to learn how to endure.**

Centuries ago, St. Francis de Sales wrote about the golden nature of affliction:

> It is said that there is a river in Boeotia wherein the fish appear golden, but taken out of those their native waters, they have the natural colour of other fishes: afflictions are so; if we look at them outside God's will, they have their natural bitterness, but he who considers them in that eternal good-pleasure, finds them all golden, unspeakably lovely and precious.[1]

The trouble is, most of us don't endure well. Oh, we try to "fix" or control. We try to clean up the mess or dull the pain (which often gives rise to addiction and more crises). We ignore it or "fake it till we make it." But endure? Are you kidding me?

Endurance is a core virtue, developed over time. It's an intentional choice to face our obstacles head-on with submitted acceptance. Then, and only then, can we learn the power of endurance.

Athletes, by choice, train their bodies to develop the muscles needed for a future reward: the gold medal, the championship ring, the golden glove. You and I are spiritual athletes. We're faced with insurmountable odds that challenge us to either resort to being spiritual couch potatoes or to endure our training with Christ. The writer of Hebrews put it this way:

> *Let us run with endurance the race God has set before us.*
> *We do this by keeping our eyes on Jesus, the champion*
> *who initiates and perfects our faith.* (Hebrews 12:1–2)

Paul, who knew more crises than most of us ever will, also spoke of endurance:

> *Forgetting the past and looking forward to what lies*
> *ahead, I press on to reach the end of the race and receive*
> *the heavenly prize for which God, through Christ Jesus, is*
> *calling us.* (Philippians 3:13–14)

Clearly, if we want to cross faith's finish line well, we need endurance. But endurance must be learned . . . and, by God's grace, that often happens through crises.

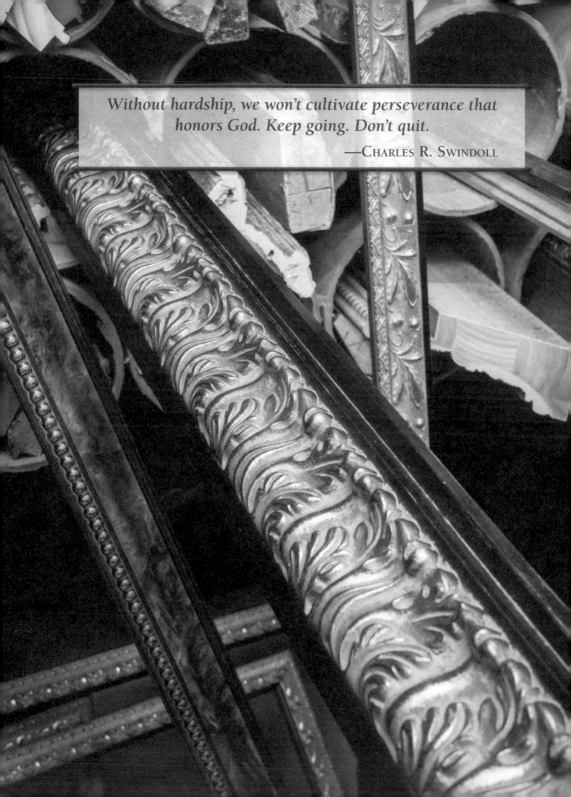

Without hardship, we won't cultivate perseverance that honors God. Keep going. Don't quit.

—CHARLES R. SWINDOLL

From Jon's seizure disorder, I've learned a few tips for reframing our crises into endurance opportunities. You can remember them by thinking on those five Ws your English teacher taught you: Who? What? When? Where? Why?

WHO endured the worst? Jesus. Perfect in every way, Jesus still had to endure mistreatment, injustice, torture, and eventually death. God allowed these horrid events so that every person who believes in Jesus as Savior can receive forgiveness of sins and eternal life. Further, Hebrews 5:8 tells us: "Even though Jesus was God's Son, he learned obedience from the things he suffered."

1. Read Isaiah 53:3–5 and ask yourself, *Can Jesus identify with me? How?*

WHAT has happened that has not already passed through the hands and heart of God? Life can be cruel, impossible, unfixable, pathetic, and unfair. To endure, we must remember God has a purpose for our pain, a reason for our suffering, and a reward for our faithfulness.

2. Write out Psalm 56:8 and circle the word *my* each time it appears. As you do, ask the Lord to speak to you about His care for you.

WHEN will our suffering be over? When will God provide? When will this or that happen? Examine those questions: Who's at the center? God or us? "When?" is a question about relief, not endurance. If our goal is to cultivate enduring, Christlike character, we must remove that question. **Remember:** God isn't limited to human time. Therefore, "when" can't be our focus.

3. **Read Isaiah 46:9–10. What does this passage tell you about God's relationship to time?**

WHERE is God? Oh, how the Enemy loves for us to ask this question! Let me assure you: Though you may feel abandoned, God hasn't left. Don't trust your feelings when they tell you otherwise. Return to the truth.

4. **Read Jesus' words in John 10:28–30. Who or what can snatch you from the Father's hand? Now ask yourself:** *WHERE am I running? Toward or away from God?*

WHY? Perhaps no other question is asked more often. I've asked it a thousand times; maybe you're asking it right now. I've learned two things about "Why?" First, I don't think any answer satisfies when we're hurting. Second, it assumes there's someone to blame. To seize the golden opportunity suffering provides, we must stop looking for someone to hold responsible and instead keep our eyes on Jesus. If we truly believe God is all He says He is, we can be content with never receiving answers.

5. Read Psalm 131:1–2 and then consider: *Do I have this type of contentment deep in my soul? What leads me to answer this way?*

I can't cure my son's seizures. We can't change what God allows. However, we're called to seek wisdom and direction from our heavenly Father through *whatever* He permits. Whenever I have to hold my son's head and wait out his seizures, I need God's peace more than answers. My guess is your need is the same. God provides that peace and abundantly more for me . . . He will do the same for you.

Reframing Crises

We can rejoice, too, when we run
into problems and trials,
for we know that they help us
develop endurance.
And endurance develops strength of
character,
and character strengthens our
confident hope of salvation.

Romans 5:3–4

Stepping into the Process

- How have you responded to what God has allowed in your life?

- Are you willing to learn to endure? What question will be the hardest to release in the process? (That's where you'll need to find support and form new daily habits. Ask the Lord to provide you with safe, wise friends who have endured well.)

- Have you seized the golden opportunities God has provided you through life's shocking surprises? How?

- What opportunities might God want you to pursue in helping others develop endurance?

Notes

Chapter Nine

The Eternal Spring: Reframing Hope

Isn't our God bigger than what
we experience on earth? He must be,
or we are doomed.

Her husband softly kissed her forehead, then let go of her hand as the nurses rolled her hospital bed into the operating room. For six hours, her family waited . . . and waited . . . .

Down hospital hallways in every country; in classrooms, courtrooms, and counseling centers; on elementary-school playgrounds and university campuses, we all instinctively cling to the same thread when life starts to unravel: *hope*.

But do we hold to the correct definition? A quick search of *hope* on the Internet produced the following results:

- A man claiming to be a physician selling hope to cancer patients through a magical, cure-all pill

- A how-to article assuring readers that hope would never run dry if they followed ten simple steps

- Chat groups galore offering hope for people enduring failing marriages, physical ailments, strained family relationships, and everything else you can think of—even groups for atheists

The trouble with all these examples is that the hope they offer is based on circumstances, people, products, and experiences. They represent what many believe hope is: an expectant, optimistic anticipation that something good *will* happen based on what we do. If we work hard, pray long, take care, be smart, and simply believe, we're guaranteed a return on our investment, right?

Not necessarily.

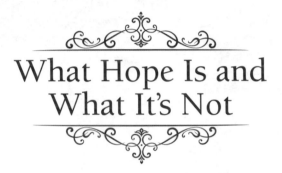

What Hope Is and What It's Not

Who hasn't heard these (mis)interpretations of Scripture?

- **Romans 8:28**: "God causes everything to work together for the good of those who love God."
  Misinterpretation: "Trust God and life will be good—at least better than without Him."

- **Proverbs 22:6**: "Direct your children onto the right path, and when they are older, they will not leave it."
  Misinterpretation: "Follow this guaranteed formula, and you'll produce spiritually devout kids."

- **The biblical testimonies** of Joseph, David, Job, Esther, and others who endured hard times, clung to God, and later experienced good things
  Misinterpretation: "If I endure, then—KABOOM!—God will give me a happily ever after!"

Formulas? Returns on investments? Sounds more like the perfect setup for total disillusionment than real hope—the kind of hope that springs eternal when we have nothing left to give and no more left to lose.

Sadly, many of us base our hope on something other than God's truth. Then, when our thread breaks, we're baffled and blame God. Real hope is the difference between surviving and thriving, no matter our circumstances. Because hope is so critical, it's vital we have a correct understanding of it. Let's begin with what hope is *not*. Christian hope does not mean:

- I will have fewer physical, emotional, or mental challenges.

- I will be financially successful.

- I will be healed from pain and disease.

- I will have perfect kids who grow up to be healthy and love Jesus.

- I will have a loving, lifelong marriage.

- I will be able to follow my dreams and know my purpose without setbacks.

Read that list again. Where's the focus? On "me" and on earthly results! This kind of hope says, "*I* am guaranteed a better life because God is on *my* side." Sounds like preschoolers arguing: "My dad is bigger than your dad! Na-na-na-na-na-na!" Sometimes, we childishly believe that God *owes* us a better life because we've offered Him our trust. At best, that's entitlement—the polar opposite of hope.

Ultimately, hope is grounded and grown, established and ensured, in ONE choice. It's a choice offered to every person: **to believe God and actively participate in whatever He allows**, regardless of what we feel, experience, lose, gain, or see in our day-to-day lives.

Read that again slowly and write a list of people to whom hope is offered and how and why it's offered:

Often, we think we have hope only when things work out for our *earthly* comfort—when our pain is relieved, our relationships reconciled, our endeavors applauded, or our investments returned. (After all, the opposite is the world's definition of *hopeless*.) Scripture, however, *never* guarantees an easy path. Instead, God's Word promises His presence *through* every circumstance. Jesus Himself told us to expect trouble:

> "*Here on earth you will have many trials and sorrows.*
> *But take heart, because I have overcome the world.*"
> (John 16:33)

> *Faith is seeing the invisible and believing the unbelievable so that you might achieve the impossible.*
>
> —Charles R. Swindoll

When we abide in Jesus, we can "take heart"—hope!—even when our *situation* remains unchanged. We know things won't be this way <u>forever</u> because we hope in the One who has overcome the world.

Hope and faith go hand in hand, supporting one another. "Faith shows the reality of what we hope for; it is the evidence of things we cannot see" (Hebrews 11:1). In other words, to have faith is to be assured of what we hope for—***what will be accomplished in eternity***. To have hope, then, is to completely surrender our lives into God's hands and trust Him to prepare us for that eternity, even through the worst of circumstances.

For each passage below, note the circumstances described and how God's presence, promises, and provisions produced and provided hope.

1. Matthew 5:1–11

2. John 11:1–44

3. 2 Corinthians 12:1–10

Remember that family I mentioned at the beginning of this chapter? That was *my* husband, *my* family waiting through *my* long surgery . . . and as it turns out, *my* very long, painful recovery. To this day, the pain continues; so does recovery. Did God let me down because I prayed for healing and yet the pain continues? *No.* It's taken me decades to understand: *Pain depletes my earthly strength, driving me to a dependence on Him that I would've never known if given relief.* God has been and continues to be faithful. On this earth, I may never be free of pain. But faith assures me that relief awaits me in eternity because I have placed my hope in Jesus.

I am waiting, pleading, yearning for God to unfold His will. But in the waiting, I choose daily, hourly, minute-by-minute to believe and actively participate in whatever God allows—separate from what I feel, experience, lose, gain, or see in my day-to-day life. Isn't our God bigger than what we experience on earth? He must be, or we are doomed.

God has given me two mentors who, from their wrestling with Him, have learned and shared two mottos I've found essential to reframing hope. Perhaps they will help you too:

- **Sometimes God allows what He hates in order to accomplish what He loves.** That means if our children are abducted, abused, or assaulted . . . if we experience divorce, death, suffering, injustice, unimaginable evil, or our deepest fears, our **hope** must be that God has allowed this pain so we might lean into Him.

- **God is not *almost* sovereign.** *Nothing* is outside His control; nothing surprises Him. Do you believe that? If that is true, we must choose to believe He is working for our good—even when we don't understand.

So where is *your* hope? Is it built, like the old hymn says, "on nothing less than Jesus' blood and righteousness?"[1] Take some time to identify the myths and truths you have embraced about hope. Search the Scriptures for truths that define hope and tell us where to place ours and how. (Romans is a great place to start!) Living a life of faith will continually lead us to our hope: eternal life with Jesus Christ. I assure you, once you experience hope—real, never-let-you-down HOPE—it will change *everything*.

Stepping into the Process

- What are your core values? Cultivating hope means we value patience, adaptability, dependence, and perseverance. How are these values active in your life? What other values lead to hope?

- In what ways have life's challenges brought you closer to the Lord? Or has life tossed you so far outside your comfort zone that you're harboring bitterness and anger rather than thankfulness, humility, and tenderness?

- Have you accepted God's *full* sovereignty? If so, how? If not, why?

- If you were to lose everything and everyone, would your hope remain?

Notes

Chapter Ten

It's Not What You Think: Reframing Love

Unless our fundamental understanding of love is aligned with God's definition of love, we will forever be restless and unsatisfied.

More than a decade ago, I sat on the bathroom floor helping my son with special needs clean up after using the restroom. Parenthood elects us to all kinds of unexpected, unpleasant responsibilities. At that time, in order to focus on my son's needs, I had stepped down from teaching Bible studies, speaking at conferences, attending seminary, and doing all the "spiritual" things I *thought* God needed me to do. On that particularly rough day, I resented the all-consuming responsibilities of raising a child with many needs. As I helped Jon, the Holy Spirit brought to mind a verse as only He can:

> *Work willingly at whatever you do, as though you were working for the Lord rather than for people.*
> (Colossians 3:23)

I repeated the last phrase over and over: "for the Lord rather than for people" . . . "for the Lord rather than for people."

Sometimes God brings Scripture to mind in beautiful ways, but this verse pierced my heart. I began to weep. God had entrusted me with His loved and treasured child—a special child who needed a bit more support than most—and I resented that?

In that moment, God softened my heart. I began to realize I had been chosen to serve Jon with honor and respect *just as if I was serving the Lord.* I had been restless and unsatisfied because my heart was set on <u>my</u> plans, <u>my</u> loves, and <u>my</u> dreams. I was so far from understanding God's love . . . which included His unconditional care for *my* endless needs.

The Greatest of These

Here's a doozy of a question: When did you first learn about love?

I don't mean romantic love . . . or love that pop stars sing about . . . or love that makes the world go 'round. I mean the love Jesus commanded in John 15:12–13—a love that calls us to lay down our lives, let go of all earthly goods, and embrace the crosses that come our way. **I'm talking about love that saves one's soul** (Mark 8:35–36).

Amid all the many definitions of love, the one that often comes first to our minds has very little to do with the Bible's love. The love God calls us to and the "love" we come by naturally are quite different. But love is God's core teaching, His central focus. And unless our fundamental understanding of love is aligned with God's definition of love, we will forever be restless and unsatisfied.

The apostle who penned those words that pierced my heart had a lot to say about love. Sandwiched between Paul's writings on all things public in the Christian body for worship, service, teaching, and gifts (1 Corinthians 12 and 14) is the paramount passage on love: 1 Corinthians 13. Pause right now and ask the Lord to open your heart to hear His words in this passage as you never have before. Read the chapter out loud. Listen to your voice and hear what the passage is saying.

Does Paul's description of love sound like the love you've experienced? Biblical love is patient and gentle, selfless and humble, enduring and thoughtful, forgiving and flexible. "Love never gives up, never loses faith, is always hopeful, and endures through every circumstance" (1 Corinthians 13:7). **Action** lies at the core of all those attributes. Exhibiting God's love, then, is active—a verb, an act of our will to care for all others unconditionally. Such love flows only from a heart surrendered to God's will and dedicated to living according to His ways. What importance does Paul place on love?

> *If I could speak all the languages of earth and of angels,*
> *but didn't love others, I would only be a noisy gong or*
> *a clanging cymbal. If I had the gift of prophecy, and if*
> *I understood all of God's secret plans and possessed all*
> *knowledge, and if I had such faith that I could move*
> *mountains, but didn't love others, I would be nothing. If I*
> *gave everything I have to the poor and even sacrificed my*
> *body, I could boast about it; but if I didn't love others, I*
> *would have gained nothing.* (13:1–3)

We may have oratory elegance, awe-inspiring gifts, and faith that quakes the earth, but without love, it's all meaningless.

Let me challenge you, before you go any further, to schedule some time to be with the Lord and ask Him what love really is. Perhaps you were "loved" painfully—*wrongly*, in fact—which colored your perspective on love. Perhaps you've never grappled with or accepted the extravagance of God's love for you and let that truth transform your heart in a way that overflows into your actions. Perhaps you've simply never really thought about how God defines love and what role it has played in your life.

Do you realize how much God loves you? Maybe today is the day you believe it. He gave His Son to die . . . for you.

—CHARLES R. SWINDOLL

Whatever the case, go to your favorite quiet spot, take this book or your journal, your Bible, your earbuds, and something that plays music. Select some praise songs or hymns that speak about love. Then read 1 Corinthians 13 again carefully. Ask God to show you how you have understood and experienced love in the past and how it can be a positive, active verb in your life moving forward. Write down what He reveals to you.

Is it time to start reframing love in your life? To do so will take time and daily, intentional effort. If you've gone to many weddings, you've likely heard "The Love Chapter" so many times it's become cliché. Refuse to let yourself gloss over God's powerful words on love. Don't let them sound ordinary or easy. Loving others as God loves us takes hard work . . . a lot of it! If we ever ease up on that work, we run the risk of becoming so filled with ourselves—our opinions and judgments, our wants and wishes, our dreams and desires—that we might begin classifying who's lovely and who isn't—or worse, who's lovable and who isn't.

God's love isn't selective! We cannot allow our opinions, desires, and fears to deter us from fulfilling His call to love others as He loves us. Graciously, the Lord has entrusted me with a family through whom God teaches me daily what loving really means. The long process of reframing love has completely changed my perspective and infused my life with joy.

More than a decade after that day with my son, I found myself on the bathroom floor again, helping another family member recover from a

Reframing Love

"For this is how God loved the world:
He gave his one and only Son,
so that everyone who believes in him
will not perish but have eternal life.
God sent his Son into the world
not to judge the world,
but to save the world through him."

John 3:16–17

painful surgery. This time, it wasn't a resented duty; it was a respected honor. To care for others unable to care for themselves—isn't that what God does for us every moment of our lives? When we remember that, the hard work of putting God's love into action becomes nothing short of a sacred honor. And when done with a heart that serves others as though serving the Lord, it brings wonderful, abiding contentment.

Now for the hard question: How do *you* define love?

Stepping into the Process

- Has your heart been broken or betrayed by someone you once loved . . . or by someone who should have loved you? If so, how has that experience affected your ability to love and receive love today? Have you pursued the process of forgiveness?

- Have you received God's extravagant love for you? What in your life makes you answer the way you do?

- How do you love others? Do you love without judgment, or do you require people to "measure up"? Do you love to get something in return, or does your love flow out of a heart that first loves God (Luke 10:27)?

- How are you doing the hard work of loving others as though "for the Lord rather than for people" (Colossians 3:23)?

Notes

Chapter Eleven

Sitting Securely
in the Suck:
Reframing Waiting

*The truth is, we have no idea what God is doing
while we're waiting—the people and pieces He's
bringing together at just the right time for His will
to be accomplished.*

My neighborhood felt like the arctic when I stepped out for an evening walk, looking for much-needed space to breathe. Life was anything but balanced; I felt disrupted and tired. Layered in clothes, I resembled an irritated woolly mammoth roaming the frozen tundra, trying to figure out which way is north.

Balance has never been simple for me. I'm captivated by those who keep orderly calendars, have nine children, wash the sheets weekly, change the oil on time, and never lose socks in the dryer. Finding my keys without turning the house upside down is a huge win! ADHD and I have a close relationship. My family is aware of my challenges. They also know when I've crested and fallen past the tipping point. (I can tell because they talk more quietly, vacuum, and clean the kitchen.)

A few minutes into my trek, my daughter called. I tried to keep the conversation off my grumpiness and on her. But she's so intuitive . . . and I'm terrible at hiding my feelings. After about forty seconds, Ashley asked what was bugging me. I glossed over it with, "I'm just tired."

She wasn't buying it. "Mom, you need to talk. You know what Bubba says . . . 'thoughts disentangle themselves through the lips and over the fingertips.'"

"Bubba" is what my kids affectionately call my dad. When one of them pulls the "Bubba Says" card, they know I can't argue. Tears warmed my cheeks as scattered thoughts spilled out like disconnected puzzle pieces. Ashley listened quietly. She then proclaimed something my dad would be, oh, so proud of because it's related to the Marine Corps. "Mom," she said, "welcome to the suck."

Will It Ever End?

I stopped in my tracks. "The suck? What the heck is that?"

Ashley explained that the phrase "embrace the suck" surfaced in the Marine Corps during the Vietnam War. Marines in difficult situations would say to one another, "Embrace the suck." Naming those terrible circumstances helped them endure by acknowledging their hated reality and reminding them that it wouldn't last forever.

"Mom," she continued, "for whatever reason, you're in the suck, and the Lord has you there. You're going to have to wait it out with Him."

I hated that answer. Even though I've spent so much time in waiting rooms that I once considered them my home away from home, I've never been skilled at waiting. I'll never forget the hours my son with

special needs and I spent in waiting rooms in the early years of his diagnoses. Wherever we were, the waiting room looked the same—filled with tattered magazines, old toys, crying children, and tired-looking people staring at smudged, blandly painted walls. If there were windows, we watched the world whirl by—beautiful women out and about, men in pressed suits connected to cell phones. Looking outside, I would get stuck in my thoughts, somewhere between envious and anxious, wearied and worried. I felt like the waiting would never end.

I'm not much better at waiting when the "waiting room" is metaphorical. I focus on my discomfort. When that leads to misery—which it *always* does—I leap into "fixing mode." I offer the Lord my unneeded but always available opinion on what *I* think would make things better. This has NEVER gone well. Trying to take over God's work always makes a massive mess. Yet somehow, I have to keep learning: It's much better to just sit in the suck, trusting that it won't be forever. As one of my friends says, "Remember, this event or season is one event or season in a LIFETIME of events and seasons."

Does waiting seem endless to you too? Take heart! We're not the first ones to experience a long haul in the waiting room. Waiting has been a vital part of each life story since the beginning! Scripture overflows with testimonies of people who waited: Noah waited for the flood to rise and recede; Abraham and Sarah waited to welcome baby Isaac; Joshua and Caleb waited for others to believe in God's power; Esther fasted before approaching King Ahasuerus; David hid in the caves of En-gedi; Simeon looked for the Messiah; Mary and Martha longed for Jesus to come; John was banished to the island of Patmos; Jesus waited in the garden of Gethsemane. Some in Scripture waited days or weeks; others waited years and years.

Waiting on God results in learning how to rest in Him.
We learn how to rest in God when we learn how to
wait on Him.

—CHARLES R. SWINDOLL

Some of us are called to wait for a long, LONG time; it's part of a bigger story that only God can unfold at the appointed time. As humans, we focus on the ticking clock. But our God is not limited to time; He created it and operates outside of it. About the ultimate "waiting room" of anticipating Jesus' return, Peter reminded us that God's work happens outside our 24-hour-day existence:

> *But you must not forget this one thing, dear friends: A day is like a thousand years to the Lord, and a thousand years is like a day.* (2 Peter 3:8)

The truth is, <u>we have no idea what God is doing while we're waiting</u>—the people and pieces He's bringing together *at just the right time* for His will to be accomplished. While we wait, He also works in us. It's a win-win, IF we're willing to embrace the suck and worship instead of getting knotted up with worry.

The Enemy will do his best to convince us that our time waiting is time wasted. When we KNOW God has instructed us to wait, we can counteract our natural feelings of anxiety, fear, and restlessness by turning to Scripture. Read Isaiah 40:26–31. What does this passage reveal about who God is and what He accomplishes in those who wait?

I'm learning what it means to "embrace the suck"—or, to put it another way, reframe waiting. Are you too? Maybe you're waiting:

- For the doctor to call with your test results

- For your adult child who has given up all faith in God to come back around

- For money to come in so you can feed your family

- For grief to lighten its harsh grip

- For the pregnancy test to turn positive

- For your child with disabilities to fit in SOMEWHERE

- For a word of hope that things will be okay

Learning to reframe waiting is an ongoing process. Some days are better for me than others! But here are three tips I've learned:

- **Be silent (Psalm 62:1–2).** Spending time in silence shuts out the noise so we can focus on hearing God's voice. If you're bothered by silence, ask the Lord why you have resistance, irritation, or a desire to pursue distractions.

- **Be still (Psalm 46:10).** If that's uncomfortable, ask God why you struggle with stillness. Stillness forces us to examine our schedules, alter priorities, heal areas of hurt, and be fully present.

- **Be sincere (Psalm 6).** God loves for us to run to Him and be thoroughly truthful. An authentic soul has nothing to hide, gain, or do but trust that God is at work.

One more idea: music always makes the time pass more sweetly. As you embrace the suck, sing along with blind poet and hymn writer Fanny J. Crosby: "Perfect submission, all is at rest, I in my Savior am happy and blest, watching and waiting, looking above, filled with his goodness, lost in his love."[1]

Reframing Waiting

Wait patiently for the Lord.

Be brave and courageous.

Yes, wait patiently for the Lord.

Psalm 27:14

Stepping into the Process

- Make a list of events in your life that required waiting. What happened when you resisted the suck and tried to fix things? What happened when you waited and watched God's work unfold?

- How has waiting developed your character? How has waiting for God to work out His good and perfect will in you affected others?

- How can you intentionally incorporate time in your life to be silent, still, and sincere?

- Is there someone you know who's stuck in his or her own suck? How might you come alongside that person?

Chapter Twelve

What You Must Do Now: Reframing Disasters

*As I have learned to reframe my approach
to disasters each time my world has threatened to
crumble, I have been better prepared to survive—
and even thrive.*

I was 4 years old the first time the chandelier in our home began to sway like a playground swing. Time stopped as the earth rocked beneath our feet. We had just moved to Orange County in Southern California. None of us knew what to do except hang on for dear life.

The San Fernando earthquake was the biggest one I experienced while growing up. For months, aftershocks rattled our world. We learned quickly that earthquakes were part of living in California, but knowing the plates of the earth could shift at any moment didn't remove our terror. I can't forget the wildfires either. That ominous glow that annually consumed the surrounding hills, completely devouring manicured lawns and beautiful homes. Etched into my memory are the smell of burning brush, sunsets colored by gray ash, early mornings when my dad and I would wipe white dust off our cars. And the mudslides! Those moving masses of soil and debris ripped our friends' homes in half—the front parts left perfectly intact, while the backsides were torn off and taken away by mud.

Now living in Texas, watching news of the Golden State feels eerily familiar. This past year, the Thomas Fire destroyed more acreage than any other fire in California's history. Perhaps the worst part came afterward. The burnt, root-bare terrain didn't stand a chance of staying put. Boulders tumbled into living rooms; mud washed an entire neighborhood off its foundations. The wreckage swallowed up lives and land without warning. Quaint, seaside Santa Barbara County was devastated.

Because I lived in Montecito while attending Westmont College, the news scenes were so real to me. I *know* those places: a shopping center where I used to pass the time, a coastal store where I worked, hillside cafés where I ate. The people who live there will rebuild, but natural disasters will remain a part of their lives.

A Daily Survival Guide

Disasters have a way of leveling the playing field. In seconds, they rip everything from the rich and famous and the poor and lonely alike. Does anyone really care about social status when his or her whole neighborhood goes up in smoke, shakes to the ground, or slides into the sea? In an instant, we're given twenty-twenty vision to see what we value most.

Disasters strip us down to bare bones faster than anything I can think of. You may never have to come face-to-face with an earthquake, wildfire, mudslide, avalanche, hurricane, tsunami, or tornado, but there's another kind of disaster we all must contend with. By nature, our sinful condition is a disaster in waiting.

Sometimes we're one choice away from losing it all. I'm not talking about possessions. I'm talking about something far more valuable: our perspective on what is of eternal value. Unless we're firmly rooted to Christ and His truth, the force of our fleshly nature will lead to disaster. We'll be swept away by the insatiable tide of selfishness and pride. We'll live unfulfilled, believing one more thing will satisfy . . . then one more . . . and one more . . . until we're eaten up, lonely and bitter, having destroyed ourselves and those around us. Sometimes we do everything right and yet, the rains come, hurricanes hit, our health fails, and life falls apart. The reality of our fallen world is that disaster can happen at any moment to anyone.

Living on the West Coast means accepting the breathtaking beauty of nature along with the possibility of total devastation. Being human means accepting the breathtaking beauty of life along with the possibility of total devastation by sin.

There's only one way to survive every threat: a soul firmly, deeply fixed to Jesus Christ. He is all-powerful. He controls all nature. He's the only anchor strong enough to hold us in a churning sea, be it the Pacific or the tide of life. God's truth is our lifeline. Come what may, if we've placed our trust in Him and planted His Word in our hearts, we will be unshakable.

Kids in California schools practice earthquake drills. My kids in Texas practiced tornado drills. Across the country, cities and states enforce building codes and practice evacuation and recovery plans. Just like we practice lifesaving techniques for natural disasters, we must practice spiritual exercises to strengthen our resolve for inevitable days of trouble. We must reframe our perspective on disasters from something to endure to *something to be ready for*.

> *The storm will come, and if you haven't a rock to stand on, you will plunge. Jesus is that Rock.*
>
> —CHARLES R. SWINDOLL

Scripture is packed with truths we can live by today to be ready for tomorrow. I've chosen some from Proverbs 3. Think of these as "soul drills." For each, write out the verse in the space provided. Consider writing over the verse in your handwriting each day for a week. (It doesn't matter if it looks messy!) Use various colors . . . one for verbs and another for commands. Highlight, underline, or even walk as you read the verses aloud. Writing and speaking with colors and body movement help our bodies and minds integrate what we're learning and reframing.

1. **Proverbs 3:1**

Memorize Scripture so it's the first thing that comes to mind when disasters hit. It will keep you from being afraid or acting on impulse.

2. **Proverbs 3:3**

Practice kindness and faithfulness (some translations say *loyalty*). These qualities keep us firmly established, steadfast, unwavering, and devoted.

3. Proverbs 3:5–6

Put full trust in God and depend upon Him always. He will show you the way to go.

4. Proverbs 3:7a

Practice humility; don't have a know-it-all mentality.

5. Proverbs 3:7b

RUN from evil. Ask the Lord to help you see where evil may be lurking. Don't flirt with the Enemy; he'll take you down.

6. Proverbs 3:11–12

We don't like pain, but if we are to be firmly established, we must allow the Lord's discipline to transform our hearts and minds.

7. Proverbs 3:25

Don't fear disasters. By seeking wisdom, you will have peace, direction, and security amid the unexpected.

8. Proverbs 3:27–30

Honor and serve others. Purpose yourself to bring peace to every situation.

I haven't been through an earthquake in years, but I have endured other disasters. I've felt pain so deep I couldn't speak, loss so grave I didn't think I could go on, fear so huge there was no light in sight. Through these earthshaking experiences, Christ refined my character and further transformed me into His image. And as I have learned to reframe my approach to disasters each time my world has threatened to crumble, I have been better prepared to survive—and even thrive.

Throughout life, we *will* encounter challenges—a fact as certain as earthquakes, wildfires, and mudslides on the West Coast. But we aren't left without hope or help. "Soul drills" today will enable you to withstand tomorrow's adversity with strength and peace.

Reframing Disasters

"Anyone who listens to my teaching
and follows it is wise,
like a person who builds a house
on solid rock.
Though the rain comes in torrents
and the floodwaters rise
and the winds beat against that house,
it won't collapse
because it is built on bedrock."

Matthew 7:24–25

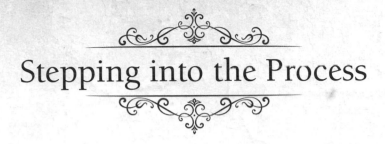

Stepping into the Process

- How have you responded to disasters, natural or otherwise, in the past? What got you through them? In what ways did you grow?

- If a natural disaster were to strike today, what loss would devastate you most? Why?

- Have you accepted that you cannot control what or whom you might lose? Are you clinging to anything or anyone instead of Christ?

- When disasters come to mind, are you overcome with anxiety? What is the root of your worry? Do you trust that God could use ANYTHING for a greater good?

- Do you avoid what is happening today by focusing on past regrets or future worries?

- What about today seems like a disaster in the making? What one or two things can you do to keep yourself unshakable?

Notes

Chapter Thirteen

When God Kicks You Out of the Nest: Reframing Your Comfort Zone

To grow as Christians . . . we must climb out of dark caverns,
survive treacherous cliffs, swim against the tide of our culture,
and wait in the freezing-cold-to-the-bone tundra . . .
often all alone.

L ife can be undeniably rugged. I was reminded of this while watching a reality show filmed in Alaska. The family homestead was in constant motion. Kids galore, parents, and grandparents fed animals, harvested fields, and stored up for winter's blast right around the corner. Certainly, no one was sittin' round the campfire—it was all work.

By the series' end, it was undeniably clear that surviving Alaska's untamed frozen tundra is for a *select* few. If I had to live there, I would become dreadfully mean, irritable, and desperate with a hacking, wet cough. Yet there's something indescribably pristine about Alaska. Snowcapped mountains wrapped with miles of thick ice. Rivers bursting with eager salmon swarming upstream to spawn. Soaring eagles sinking their claws into food for their young. It's creation at its wildest—colored canopies, wooded scents, mossy soil, mysterious icy caverns—especially delightful to behold on TV . . . while sitting in a warm home with running water and indoor plumbing.

It's one thing to *see* the wild of Alaska; it's another to *live* in it. Those who do must cultivate survival skills that are impossible to develop merely by watching TV. The same can be said about the Bible. It's one thing to *read* the Bible (which is essential); it's another to *apply* it.

The process of developing your character through a life of faith is a bit like being dropped into the wilderness of Alaska. To grow as Christians, we must learn survival skills to withstand the grueling elements. We must climb out of dark caverns, survive treacherous cliffs, swim against the tide of our culture, and wait in the freezing-cold-to-the-bone tundra . . . often all alone.

Character is beautiful. Developing character is hard.

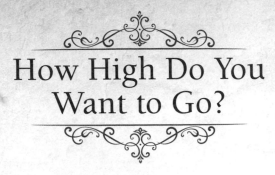

How High Do You Want to Go?

From birth, it's "survival of the fittest" for Alaskan eaglets. Sibling rivalry knocks out the weakest ones; the few who survive are in for a whole new game of "catch and release." When it's time, the mother kicks her offspring out of the nest. That's right—she punts her little baby out with one goal: to teach it to fly. The eaglet screams and squeals, flopping its downy feathers in the frosty air without much luck. In the nick of time, Mama Eagle swoops down and catches the terrified ball of fluff. These flying lessons usually last several hours—punt and swoop, punt and swoop—until FINALLY punt and *fly*. It's a painful process to watch! But what seems so cruel is <u>necessary</u> for the eaglet to survive and grow into a strong, adult eagle—among the most noble and breathtaking of God's creations in the sky.

Has God put you through flying lessons lately? Have you been punted out of your "nest"—your comfort zone that keeps you insulated from life's harsh realities? The Christian life is NOT for the faint of heart! Your wings of faith will never grow strong and thick if you stay in your comfy nest. But there is *nothing* fun about the free fall—it's downright terrifying. Yet our God promises to swoop down, catch our flailing lives, and carry us in the warm, safe shelter of His wings where He will renew our strength.

Scripture repeatedly pictures God as a strong, faithful Father who carries us and shelters us with His mighty wings. Read the following passages and note the ways God is described. (Better yet, if you're inclined and inspired, draw a visual reminder of the truths these verses share!)

1. Exodus 19:4

2. Deuteronomy 32:11

3. Ruth 2:11–12

4. Psalm 36:5–7

5. Psalm 63:6–8

6. Psalm 91:3–4

Even more faithful than Mama Eagle, God shows up every time. BUT He will not allow us to stay in that comfortable place indefinitely. The Christian life requires that we grow and change—*so we can soar.*

The question is: how badly do you want to fly? The Lord will lift you on wings like eagles, **but YOU have to get out of the nest**. That means you must reframe your understanding of your comfort zone— What is it? What's it for? *What is it keeping you from?* There's nothing inherently wrong with a comfort zone. God intentionally brings us into ours for safety, refreshment, and renewal. But He doesn't intend for us to stay there . . . and usually, we have no intention of leaving!

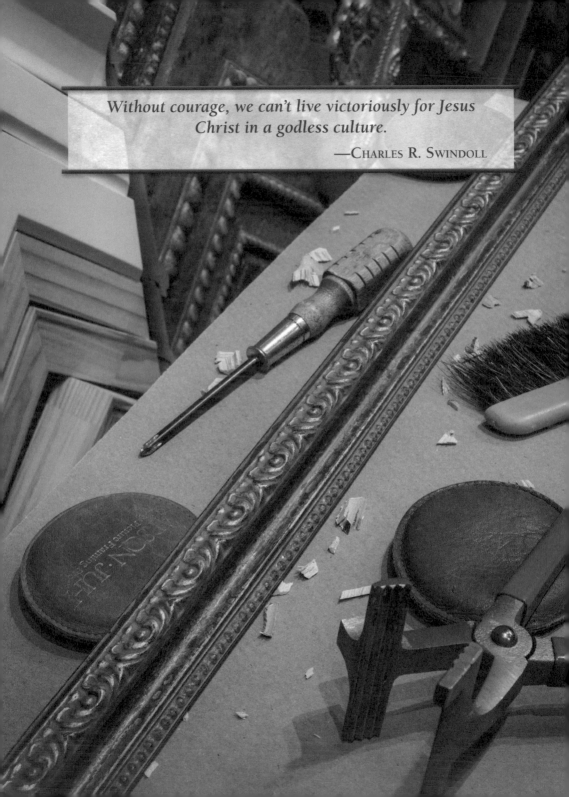

> *Without courage, we can't live victoriously for Jesus Christ in a godless culture.*
>
> —CHARLES R. SWINDOLL

Leaving our comfort zones isn't easy. It's not how we're "wired." Our brains get set in their ways, and remapping our neurological pathways requires focused engagement. For most of us, leaving our comfort zones isn't fun either. (Even the most adventurous have their limits. Perhaps skydiving is no big deal to you, but talking to a cashier about Jesus makes you break out in hives!) I can't even promise that leaping out of the nest will be as *instantly* rewarding as your first plunge off the high dive or that first drop on a rollercoaster. Learning to fly is an arduous, heart-pumping journey. But the hard-earned rewards last a lifetime . . . and longer.

If you're terrified to risk the leap, I understand! I've always had an adventurous spirit, but "flying" with more faith than fear is an ongoing challenge for me. I have to reframe what I <u>know</u> about the Lord with what I <u>feel</u> about my circumstances. I ask myself regularly, *Do I believe God is good? Trustworthy? Sovereign?* And I affirm each little step I make to trust and release—trust and release—a little more each day.

As you begin to reframe your comfort zone, you'll see where the Lord is leading you to spread your wings and fly. **Don't be afraid to ask Him for courage.** Courage, as my dad would say, has never met its match! With courage, Abraham packed his bags for an unknown land, David picked up his sling, Deborah marched into battle, Daniel knelt in prayer, and Ruth followed Naomi. With courage, Mary gave birth to Jesus, Peter stood up at Pentecost, and Paul pressed on to Rome. Courage is what it takes to seek help, get up, keep going, or pull someone else up. Courage enables us to believe God is sovereign, and because He is, we can trust Him with everything and everyone we love—including our own comfort and safety. So ask Him to fill you with courageous faith that emboldens you to look over the edge of that nest and jump!

Reframing Your Comfort Zone

He gives power to the weak
and strength to the powerless.
Even youths will become
weak and tired,
and young men
will fall in exhaustion.
But those who trust in the Lord
will find new strength.
They will soar high on wings
like eagles.
They will run and not grow weary.
They will walk and not faint.

Isaiah 40:29–31

Remember: in all ways, Christ is our example. God the Father asked Christ the Son to leap from the comforts of heaven's nest to live with us and die for us so that we could be offered eternal life. Because He did, we have the assurance of His grace. Yes, your leap will be a free fall . . . right into the arms of the One who will save you.

Don't wait another minute. Get out of that nest! I promise; God will take you to new, indescribable vistas. From one eaglet to another, let's soar!

Stepping into the Process

- Have you ever leapt from your "nest"? What happened?

- Is God asking you to take a leap of faith now? What's keeping you from stepping out of your comfort zone? Is your comfort more important than Christ's promise to walk with you through change?

- Are you missing anything by staying safe in your "nest"? Have you ever considered that by refusing to step out, you may be hurting others or holding yourself back from what God has for you?

- Do you believe that God is trustworthy, good, sovereign? What evidence in your life shows that to be true?

- Whom can you ask to pray for you to have the courage you need to soar?

Notes

Chapter Fourteen

Triggers, Traps, and Truth Bombs: Reframing Security

*When we respond with fear,
we choose to habitually follow broken, self-focused
methods that don't work and hurt others.*

One summer, all my "best thinking" led to some tearful conversations with my older two kids, Ashley and Austin. Apparently, there was a disconnect . . . and it wasn't on their end.

It all started in May. My stepson got married, and Austin came home from college to work and take classes online. We planned for both excitedly. What we didn't plan on was identity theft, which led to documents galore; no Internet or phones; and a thorough rewiring of our home. I admit—I was a little uptight. Okay, so I was Squidward Tentacles from *SpongeBob SquarePants* on a very bad day . . . for days . . . which turned into weeks . . . which turned into the whole summer.

The chaos played right into the areas where I'm most fragile: mistrust and anxiety connected to past domestic abuse in my adulthood; nightmares; and challenges with focus. Instead of "letting go and letting God," I tried to control everything. (Control is tricky. It can disguise itself as "being responsible" or "doing what we HAVE to.") My tongue became a laser, firing upon the smallest irritation. My mind focused on perception rather than reality. I stopped laughing and being the silly mom and wife I usually am. Instead, I became the hypersensitive, demanding, drive-you-nuts kind of person everyone avoids.

In my desperation to protect myself, I was hurting those I love the most . . . and I had no clue. That's what self-focus, fear, and worry do: blind us.

Near the end of the summer, Ashley and her husband came to visit. Our typical laughter was missing. In our home, surrounded by security teams and cameras, she asked, "Mom, can we go into your room? I need you." Within moments, her tears began to tumble. "Mom, you've always told us to tell you the truth, so I'm going to, but I don't know how you'll take it. It's a truth bomb, but I need you to hear me."

It *was* a bomb—the kind that can blow up our self-centered worlds *if* we're committed to listening. A truth bomb reveals our blinding, binding attitudes and actions. It can be painful because it rocks our comfort zones and sheds light on how we're hurting ourselves and others. Without knowing what Ashley had said, that same week, Austin expressed similar emotions. When my kids come to me with enough love to speak hard truths, and those truths are similar, I know my kids are not the problem.

Choosing to Be Free

Have you noticed how God orchestrates seemingly unrelated things to communicate His longing for us to hear and trust Him? That week, I encountered my kids' words, a book I happened to pick up, a Sunday-morning message, and a podcast that all mentioned John 10:10:

> *"The thief's purpose is to steal and kill and destroy. My purpose is to give them a rich and satisfying life."*

God got my attention! Make no mistake, the Enemy is determined to destroy us. A thief cares foremost about his or her wants. If you've been the victim of theft, you know the experience not only costs you in possessions; it also robs you of security, clarity, and confidence. A thief leaves a trail of loss, confusion, and fear. It's the same with the Devil. He wants to create chaos and confusion, steal our joy, and distract us from a godly focus. If he could, the Devil would rob us of all our trust in Christ, leaving us plagued with doubts about who God is and His care for us.

In my case, a literal thief had stolen from me. The experience served as a trigger—it opened the door for Satan to steal what's of more value: my sense of security in Christ. If that security is shaken, the vibrations go out to every person and area of my life. Like shrapnel spewing from an enemy's bomb, my reaction to the trigger had caused painful damage. I knew that I needed to reframe. That started with going to the One who is an expert on all things, including Enemy territory.

We all have "triggers"— sights, smells, images, experiences, expressions, and anything else that looks or feels like something that has hurt us in the past. When a core need such as safety, acceptance, love, nutrition, or being valued, cared for, and understood has been unmet or damaged, our brains are wired to avoid the experience again at all costs. Anything we perceive as a threat is a trigger. When that trigger fires, it stirs up the pain we've buried. We're shot back in time, and most likely, we don't even realize it.

Identifying our triggers is critical, because how we respond to them can be the difference between an abundant life and one stripped of God's good gifts. Once we've identified our triggers, we must examine our choices, decisions, and direction. Will we respond with fear, tumbling back into the pain and traps of the past? Or will we recognize the triggers and, with Christ as our healer, move forward?

When we respond with fear, we choose to habitually follow broken, self-focused methods that don't work and hurt others. Trapped in the maze of self-protection, we make a dangerous choice: to believe in our fear rather than reality. Worse, we choose to believe that *our* resources, agenda, and emotional defense mechanisms will keep us more secure than God's.

Our brains and bodies keep score of what has hurt us. God created in us ways to survive trauma, but if that trauma is not addressed, it compromises how we think, feel, and go about life. Decades into the healing process, a new trigger can surface, revealing a lie we didn't realize we had been believing, another wound we didn't know had been festering, and another area in which we have not grounded our security in Jesus. Every trigger we don't investigate robs us of the joy and freedom Christ gives.

God reveals the truth to help us focus on reality.
We want what's real. So does He.

—CHARLES R. SWINDOLL

Are you aware of triggers in your life? Perhaps they're alerting you to seek God's help for healing! Take some time to consider your triggers and what you have believed about your past pain in contrast to your present reality and what God's Word promises to those who choose to walk in His truth.

Trigger/Perception	God's Truth

The next time a trigger fires, be armed with the truth! **Remember:** the battle we fight is not one of flesh and blood, and as a Christian you have all you need to win (Ephesians 6:10–18).

Reframing security is a lifelong process. It's also a choice. Until we're willing to listen to those who really love us and long for real relationships with us, we'll remain trapped in fear, reliving the hurt from the past. A truth bomb is a gift! It can blow up all the false thinking and self-protecting habits we've developed due to pain. God can use that pain for a greater purpose if we allow Him.

I'm so grateful for the truth bombs my children dropped on me! Have all my problems resolved? No. Will I face identity theft again? Maybe. Is my family more valuable than false beliefs? ABSOLUTELY! So I began making changes. It's been hard and uncomfortable. But to live *abundantly* with Christ and those I love, I'm called to embrace my fragility, release control, seek support, and rest in the security of Christ. So are you.

The truth, my friend, will set you free. Secure yourself fully to the One who is sovereign. He longs to give you rest. Ask Him to help you know the truth, believe the truth, and live freely in it.

Reframing Security

You will keep in perfect peace
all who trust in you,
all whose thoughts are fixed on you!
Trust in the LORD always,
for the LORD GOD is the eternal Rock.

Isaiah 26:3–4

Stepping into the Process

- Have you experienced unmet needs or trauma? As a result, do you dismiss or overrespond to painful things today?

- Has your past caused you to believe lies that are impacting your life today? Have you named those lies and spoken the truth about them out loud?

- What "triggers" you? Are you willing to address those things and seek healing?

- What do you need to do to find support? Individual, couples, or family counseling? Journaling? Scripture memory with a trusted friend?

Chapter Fifteen

Is It Time to
Come Clean?
Reframing Your Identity

*There's only one voice—one single voice—that defines you:
the voice of the One who made you.*

This is our last chapter, so it's time to come clean: I wish I had superpowers.

Not run-of-the-mill flying or X-ray vision but superpowers to meet all the expectations of others. Powers to be the perfect mother, as well as a sexy, fun wife, an excellent employee, and a loving friend. Powers to perfectly balance the responsibilities of caring for a son with disabilities, making unforgettable dinners, volunteering at Thanksgiving, being an angel at Christmas, staying a size 2, and winning "yard of the month" . . . all with a lovely smile.

Is that too much to ask?

Recently, I searched for "perfect woman" on the Internet. My screen lit up with a bazillion links! I clicked on one. It turned out to be a page written by a man who asserted that the perfect woman changes with age. Now isn't that helpful? I immediately thought of hermit crabs and their shell-shedding process. As they get ready to change, they give off molting signs, called the "Pre-Molting Stages" or PMS. (Scout's honor!) They get all crabby, wanting to be left alone as they leave the small shell they've outgrown and move into better, bigger digs. Next, I checked out an exhausting six-part outline with to-do lists on how to become the perfect woman. Another site combined thirteen different celebrity facial features to make the "perfect" face.

Sadly, in all my reading, I found little difference between Christian opinions and secular ones. From *Cosmopolitan* to Christian magazines I won't name, the results were disheartening and empty, unapologetically brash, and excessively conflicted.

So what do we do with the tension of being flawed humans but longing to be perfect superhumans?

The One (and Only) Voice We Should Listen To

New York Times best-selling author David Brooks sums up our human thinking about success: "When we think about making a difference or leading a life with purpose, we often think of achieving something external—performing some service that will have an impact on the world, creating a successful company, or doing something for the community."[1] Richard Rohr notes that the "be perfect" pressure is even more intense in religious circles: "Much of organized religion . . . tends to be peopled by folks who have a mania for some ideal order, which is never true, so they are seldom happy or content." Rohr's take on what religious leaders often teach? "If you are not perfect, then *you* are doing something wrong."[2]

OUCH.

At the heart of the gospel is Jesus' great, sacrificial love that led Him to die for us *because we are not perfect and cannot be on our own.* I know that—and yet, I still long for those superpowers and get down on myself when I turn up human.

Why is being human so hard? Perhaps because we're bombarded with messages that define who we are by what we can accomplish rather than by the One who created us. It's taken a tremendous amount of effort, but I'm learning to tune out the countless individuals, blogs, videos, magazines, books, and social media sites that scream the wrong message about a person's value. Honestly, sometimes I have to tune out my own voice too. Because—and don't miss this:

> *There's only one voice—one single voice—that defines you: the voice of the One who made you.*

God knows you. He loves you. He created every part of you: "In the image of God he created them; male and female he created them" (Genesis 1:27). YOU are part of God's crowning creative work. Who you are, your existence and essence, is defined by God and God alone.

Growing up, I must've heard my dad say every week: "Colleen, in life, you must 1. Know who you are, 2. Like who you are, and 3. Be who you are." I don't know if my dad knew how much I would need that powerful truth, but I'm certain God did. Throughout my life, I've struggled deeply with depression, fear, mindfulness, self-worth, and shattered dreams. I've felt insignificant and unable to balance life's responsibilities. I've learned these are symptoms of a deeper conflict— an uncertain, unstable identity. Pursuing unattainable superpowers is just another attempt to hide feelings of insignificance. Learning this has set me on a lifelong quest of reframing my identity so it is rooted in Christ alone. The first step in that ongoing process? Coming clean with myself about what I believe about God and what God says about me.

If you want to rid yourself of unrealistic expectations, you HAVE to hear God's voice louder than your own. You must start with what you choose to believe about God . . . *because what you believe about God determines what you believe about you.*

This week, read and meditate on the following passages and questions.

1. **Psalm 139: Do you believe God created you—that His fingerprints are all over you? Do you believe He knows and loves you and is with you no matter where you go or the darkness that surrounds you?**

2. **Ephesians 2:1–10 and 1 John 4:9–10: How much "doing" is required to receive God's love? Are you willing to accept that God's love is founded on HIS choice to love you and NOTHING you do or say can change what HE chooses?**

God knows everything about us, but He loves us still.
That's what makes grace amazing.

—CHARLES R. SWINDOLL

3. Matthew 5:1–11 and Galatians 5:16–26: Do you believe God defines you by your roles and responsibilities or by your character? What do you think God values most in you?

Let me give you those three points from my dad again, but this time as questions. Sorting out these questions is essential to reframing your identity so that it is placed firmly in Christ alone. ***Doing that is essential to every other issue you will ever need to reframe.*** Your work on these questions will help you more than anything I could write in this book. So take a deep breath and come clean with yourself.

Examine one question a week, not all three at once. Proverbs tells us life flows from our hearts, so take time to dive deeply into these questions (Proverbs 4:23).

1. Do you know who you are?

2. Do you like who you are?

3. Are you being who you are?

If you're tired of feeling conflicted, exhausted, and "less than," let me challenge you: do the hard work of reframing your identity in Christ. It's worth it to feel comfortable and confident in your own skin and in the beautiful, messy process of becoming like Christ. Come clean with the Lord about who you've tried to be, who you want to be, and who you have believed Him to be. Ask Him to reveal His truth to you and walk you through the process of reframing.

My son with so many disabilities is valued just as greatly as the person who seems to do it all, be it all, and have it all. There is no other Jon. There is no other YOU! You are exactly who God made you to be—someone you can know . . . like . . . and be free to be.

Reframing Your Identity

You are a chosen people.
You are royal priests, a holy nation,
God's very own possession.
As a result, you can show others
the goodness of God,
for he called you out of the darkness
into his wonderful light.
"Once you had no identity
as a people;
now you are God's people.
Once you received no mercy;
now you have received God's mercy.

1 Peter 2:9–10

Stepping into the Process

- If asked to provide a bio about you, what would you write? Does your description contain more about what you *do* or who you *are*? What needs to shift?

- Are you believing any messages that aren't rooted in Christ? How dependent are you on the Bible vs. social media, magazines, or what others say you need to do, say, or be?

- Do you struggle with depression brought on by circumstances that make you question your value? What steps can you take to help ward off those episodes? Have you tried Scriptures taped to your mirror, calling a friend, connecting with a counselor, or seeing a physician for medication needs? Do these suggestions make you feel weak or empowered—why?

- What are some practical ways you can cultivate in your life one or two qualities from Jesus' Sermon on the Mount (Matthew 5)?

Notes

Endnotes

Chapter Six

1. Ronald E. Riggio, "There's Magic in Your Smile: How Smiling Affects Your Brain," *Psychology Today*, June 25, 2012, https://www.psychologytoday.com/us/blog/cutting-edge-leadership /201206/there-s-magic-in-your-smile (accessed May 2, 2018).

Chapter Eight

1. St. Francis de Sales, *Treatise on the Love of God*, BibleHub, http://biblehub.com/library/francis/treatise_on_the_love_of_god /chapter_ii_that_the_union.htm (accessed May 9, 2018)

Chapter Nine

1. Edward Mote, "My Hope Is Built on Nothing Less," (1834).

Chapter Eleven

1. Fanny J. Crosby, "Blessed Assurance," (1873).

Chapter Fifteen

1. David Brooks, *The Road to Character* (New York: Random House, 2015), 9.

2. Richard Rohr, *Falling Upward: A Spirituality for the Two Halves of Life* (San Francisco: Jossey-Bass, 2011), 7, 60–61.

REFRAMING
MINISTRIES
with Colleen Swindoll Thompson

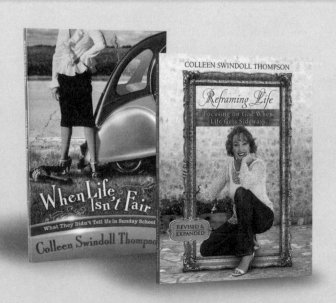

Reframing means choosing to look at life through a different lens.

These resources and more from Reframing Ministries will help you jumpstart your reframing journey today.

Reframing Ministries

Reframing Ministries is an outreach of Insight for Living Ministries, featuring Colleen Swindoll Thompson's articles, books, videos, and interviews with guest experts. Connect with Colleen on Facebook, Instagram, Twitter, Tumblr, and other popular media platforms, and find resources and support at **www.reframingministries.com**.

The Reframing Ministries Web site is packed with helpful tools for your reframing journey.

- Read articles by Colleen and inspirational quotes.

- View video interviews with experts on mental health issues, surviving tragedy, parenting children with special needs, coping with loss, and many more subjects. Guests include well-known Christian speakers such as Chuck Swindoll, Ken and Joni Eareckson Tada, Patsy Clairmont, Philip Yancey, Greg Laurie, Carlos Whittaker, and others.

- Download podcasts of Colleen's interviews so you can listen on the go.

- Peruse lists of vital resources for caregivers, pastors, parents, and anyone who needs help connecting with ministries that can make a difference.

www.reframingministries.com

Insight for Living Ministries